AMERICA'S **HEALTHY COOKING**

pasta

AMERICA'S HEALTHY COOKING

pasta

JG
PRESS

Published by World Publications Group, Inc.
455 Somerset Avenue
North Dighton, MA 02764
www.wrldpub.net

All photographs courtesy of Sunset Books

ISBN 1-57215-418-7

Editors: Joel Carino and Emily Zelner
Designer: Lynne Yeamans/Lync
Production Director: Ellen Milionis

Printed and bound in China by SNP Leefung Printers Limited.

1 2 3 4 5   06 05 03 02

pasta

pasta pie

preparation time: about 45 minutes

PASTA PIE:

1/2 cup nonfat milk

1 teaspoon cornstarch

2 large eggs

6 large egg whites

3/4 cup shredded part-skim mozzarella cheese

1/4 cup grated Parmesan cheese

2 tablespoons chopped fresh oregano
 or 1 1/2 teaspoons dried oregano

2 cloves garlic, minced or pressed

1/4 teaspoon salt

1/8 teaspoon crushed red pepper flakes

3 cups cold cooked spaghetti

1 teaspoon vegetable oil

TOMATO CREAM SAUCE:

1 large can (about 28 oz.) diced tomatoes

1/2 cup reduced-fat sour cream

2 or 3 cloves garlic, peeled

2 teaspoons chopped fresh thyme
 or 1/2 teaspoon dried thyme

1 teaspoon sugar, or to taste

Salt and pepper

GARNISH

Oregano sprigs and fresh oregano leaves

1 In a large bowl, combine milk and cornstarch; beat until smoothly blended. Add eggs and egg whites and beat well. Stir in mozzarella cheese, Parmesan cheese, chopped oregano, minced garlic, the 1/4 teaspoon salt, and red pepper flakes. Add pasta to egg mixture; lift with 2 forks to mix well. Set aside.

2 Place a 9-inch-round baking pan (do not use a nonstick pan) in oven while it heats to 500°. When pan is hot (after about 5 minutes), carefully remove it from oven and pour in oil, tilting pan to coat. Mix pasta mixture again; then transfer to pan. Bake on lowest rack of oven until top of pie is golden and center is firm when lightly pressed (about 25 minutes).

3 Meanwhile, to prepare tomato cream sauce, pour tomatoes and their liquid into a food processor or blender. Add sour cream, peeled garlic, thyme, and sugar; whirl until smoothly puréed. Season to taste with salt and pepper, set aside. Use at room temperature.

4 When pie is done, spread about 3/4 cup of the sauce on each of 4 individual plates. Cut pie into 4 wedges; place one wedge atop sauce on each plate. Garnish with oregano sprigs and leaves. Offer remaining sauce to drizzle over pie.

makes 4 servings

per serving: 411 calories, 26 g protein, 47 g carbohydrates, 14 g total fat, 133 mg cholesterol, 782 mg sodium

COOK PASTA CORRECTLY: In general, you'll need about 3 quarts of water for 8 ounces of fresh or dry pasta, about 6 quarts for a pound. Once the water has come to a boil, add the pasta; leave the pan uncovered, then begin timing after the water has resumed a full boil. Begin taste-testing before the recommended cooking time is up. Pasta should be cooked al dente—literally, "to the tooth," or tender but still firm to bite. As soon as pasta reaches that stage, drain it in a colander; then serve at once or keep warm in a warm bowl.

ravioli with gorgonzola

preparation time: about 40 minutes

2 packages (about 9 oz. *each*) fresh low-fat
cheese-filled ravioli

1/4 cup finely chopped onion

2 cloves garlic, minced or pressed

4 teaspoons cornstarch

1 cup nonfat milk

1/2 cup half-and-half

1/2 cup vegetable broth

2 ounces Gorgonzola or other blue-veined
cheese, crumbled

1/4 teaspoon dried thyme

1/4 teaspoon dried marjoram

1/4 teaspoon rubbed sage

1/8 teaspoon ground nutmeg

1 teaspoon dry sherry, or to taste

Finely shredded lemon peel

Salt and pepper

1. In a 6- to 8-quart pan, bring about 4 quarts water to a boil over medium high heat. Stir in ravioli, separating any that are stuck together, reduce heat and boil gently, stirring occasionally, until pasta is just tender to bite, 4 to 6 minutes. (Or cook pasta according to package directions.) Drain well, return to pan, and keep warm.

2. While pasta is cooking, combine onion, garlic, and 1 tablespoon water in a wide nonstick frying pan. Cook over medium-high heat, stirring often, until onion is soft (3 to 4 minutes); add water, 1 tablespoon at a time, if pan appears dry. Remove from heat.

3. Smoothly blend cornstarch with 2 tablespoons of the milk. Add cornstarch mixture, remaining milk, half-and-half, and broth to pan. Return to medium-high heat and bring to a boil, stirring. Reduce heat to low and add cheese, thyme, marjoram, sage, and nutmeg; stir until cheese is melted. Remove pan from heat and stir in sherry.

4. Spoon sauce over pasta; mix gently. Spoon pasta onto individual plates; sprinkle with lemon peel. Season to taste with salt and pepper.

makes 6 servings

per serving: 315 calories, 15 g protein, 40 g carbohydrates, 10 g total fat, 69 mg cholesterol, 545 mg sodium

rotini with broccoli ricotta

preparation time: about 40 minutes

12 ounces dried rotini or other
corkscrew-shaped pasta

2 tablespoons olive oil

5 green onions, thinly sliced

1 pound broccoli flowerets,
cut into bite-size pieces

1 1/2 cups part-skim ricotta cheese

Freshly grated Parmesan cheese

Coarsely ground pepper

1. Bring 12 cups water to a boil in a 5- to 6-quart pan over medium-high heat. Stir in pasta and cook just until tender to bite (8 to 10 minutes); or cook according to package directions. Meanwhile, heat oil in a wide nonstick frying pan over medium-high heat. Add onions and cook, stirring, for 1 minute. Add broccoli and continue to cook, stirring, until bright green (about 3 minutes). Pour in 1/4 cup water and bring to a boil; reduce heat, cover, and simmer until broccoli is tender-crisp (about 5 minutes).

2. Drain pasta well, reserving 1/4 cup of the water. Place in a serving bowl. Add vegetables and ricotta. Mix thoroughly but gently; if too dry, stir in enough of the reserved water to moisten. Offer Parmesan and pepper to add to taste.

makes 4 servings

per serving: 540 calories, 25 g protein, 75 g carbohydrates, 16 g total fat, 29 mg cholesterol, 149 mg sodium

artichoke pesto pasta

preparation time: about 30 minutes

1/4 cup pine nuts

1 can (about 10 oz.) artichoke hearts in water, drained

1/2 cup freshly grated Parmesan cheese

3 ounces Neufchâtel or nonfat cream cheese

1/4 cup diced onion

1 tablespoon Dijon mustard

1 clove garlic, minced or pressed

1/8 teaspoon ground nutmeg

3/4 cup vegetable broth

1 pound dried fettuccine

1/4 cup minced parsley

1/4 teaspoon crushed red pepper flakes

1 Toast pine nuts in a small frying pan over medium heat, shaking pan often, until golden (about 3 minutes). Remove from pan and set aside.

2 Combine artichokes, Parmesan, Neufchâtel, onion, mustard, garlic, nutmeg, and 1/2 cup of the broth in a food processor or blender. Whirl until blended. Set aside.

3 Bring 16 cups water to a boil in a 6- to 8-quart pan over medium-high heat. Stir in pasta and cook just until tender to bite (8 to 10 minutes); or cook according to package directions. Drain well and return to pan. Reduce heat to medium, add remaining 1/4 cup broth, and cook, lifting pasta with 2 forks, until broth is hot (about 30 seconds).

4 Transfer to a large serving bowl. Quickly add artichoke mixture, parsley, red pepper flakes, and nuts; lift with 2 forks to mix.

makes 8 servings

per serving: 307 calories, 13 g protein, 44 g carbohydrates, 9 g total fat, 66 mg cholesterol, 309 mg sodium

italian garden pasta

preparation time: about 40 minutes

12 ounces Swiss chard

1 pound dried rotini or elbow macaroni

3 tablespoons olive oil or vegetable oil

1 pound mushrooms, sliced

1 medium-size onion, chopped

3 cloves garlic, minced or pressed

1/2 cup canned vegetable broth

1/2 cup grated Parmesan cheese

1 1/2 pounds pear-shaped (Roma-type) tomatoes, chopped and drained well

1 Trim and discard discolored stem ends from chard; then rinse and drain chard. Cut stems from leaves; finely chop stems and leaves, keeping them in separate piles.

2 In a 6- to 8-quart pan, cook pasta in about 4 quarts boiling water until just tender to bite (8 to 10 minutes); or cook according to package directions. Drain well, transfer to a warm wide bowl, and keep warm.

3 While pasta is cooking, heat oil in a wide non-stick frying pan or wok over medium-high heat. When oil is hot, add chard stems, mushrooms, onion, and garlic. Cover and cook until mushrooms release their liquid and onion is tinged with brown. Add broth and chard leaves; stir until chard is just wilted (1 to 2 more minutes).

4 Pour chard-mushroom mixture over pasta, sprinkle with half the cheese, and top with tomatoes. Mix gently but thoroughly. Sprinkle with remaining Parmesan cheese.

makes 4 to 6 servings

per serving: 531 calories, 21 g protein, 84 g carbohydrates, 13 g total fat, 8 mg cholesterol, 402 mg sodium

southwestern fettuccine

preparation time: about 35 minutes

12 ounces dried fettuccine

1 can (about 15 oz.) cream-style corn

^{2}/$_3$ cup nonfat milk

1 teaspoon vegetable oil

^{1}/$_2$ teaspoon cumin seeds

1 small onion, chopped

1 large red or yellow bell pepper, seeded and cut into thin strips

1 package (about 10 oz.) frozen corn kernels, thawed and drained

1 cup (about 4 oz.) shredded jalapeño jack cheese

^{1}/$_4$ cup cilantro leaves

1 ^{1}/$_2$ to 2 cups yellow or red cherry tomatoes, cut into halves

Cilantro sprigs

Lime wedges

Salt

1 In a 5- to 6-quart pan, bring about 3 quarts water to boil over medium high heat; stir in pasta and cook until just tender to bite, 8 to 10 minutes. (Or cook pasta according to package directions.) Drain pasta well and return to pan; keep warm. While pasta is cooking, whirl cream-style corn and milk in a blender or food processor until smoothly puréed; set aside.

2 Heat oil in a wide nonstick frying pan over medium-high heat. Add cumin seeds, onion, and bell pepper. Cook, stirring often, until onion is soft (about 5 minutes); add water, 1 tablespoon at a time, if pan appears dry. Stir in cream-style corn mixture, corn kernels, and cheese. Reduce heat to medium and cook, stirring, just until cheese is melted.

3 Pour corn-cheese sauce over pasta. Add cilantro leaves; mix gently but thoroughly. Divide pasta among 4 shallow individual bowls; sprinkle with tomatoes. Garnish with cilantro sprigs. Season to taste with lime and salt.

makes 4 servings

per serving: 627 calories, 25 g protein, 104 g carbohydrates, 15 g total fat, 112 mg cholesterol, 540 mg sodium.

asparagus & pasta stir-fry

preparation time: about 25 minutes

6 ounces dried vermicelli

1 pound asparagus

2 teaspoons salad oil

1 clove garlic, minced or pressed

1 teaspoon minced fresh ginger

^{1}/$_2$ cup diagonally sliced green onions

2 tablespoons reduced sodium soy sauce

^{1}/$_8$ teaspoon crushed red pepper flakes

1 In a 4- to 6-quart pan, cook pasta in about 8 cups boiling water until just tender to bite (8 to 10 minutes); or cook according to package directions.

2 Meanwhile, snap off and discard tough ends of asparagus: then cut asparagus into 1^1/$_2$-inch slanting slices and set aside. Heat oil in a wide nonstick frying pan sir wok over medium high heat. When oil is hot, add garlic, ginger, asparagus, and onions. Stir-fry until asparagus is tender-crisp to bite (about 3 minutes). Add soy sauce and red pepper flakes; stir-fry for 1 more minute.

3 Drain pasta well, add to asparagus mixture, and stir-fry until heated through.

makes 4 to 6 servings

per serving: 167 calories, 7 g protein, 30 g carbohydrates, 3 g total fat, 0 mg cholesterol, 248 mg sodium

goat cheese & spinach pasta

preparation time: about 35 minutes

12 ounces dried spinach fettuccine

3 quarts lightly packed rinsed, drained fresh spinach leaves, cut or torn into 2-inch pieces

2/3 cup vegetable broth

8 ounces unsweetened soft fresh goat cheese (plain or flavored), broken into chunks, if possible (some types may be too soft to break)

2 cups ripe cherry tomatoes (at room temperature), cut into 1/2-inch slices

Salt and pepper

1. In a 5 to 6 quart pan, bring abut 3 quarts water to a boil over medium-high heat; stir in pasta and cook until just tender to bite, 8 to 10 minutes. (Or cook pasta according to package directions.) Stir spinach into boiling water with pasta; continue to boil until spinach is wilted (30 to 45 more seconds). Drain pasta-spinach mixture well and return to pan.

2. While pasta is cooking, bring broth to a boil in a 1-to 2-quart pan over medium-high heat. Add cheese and stir until melted; remove from heat.

3. Spoon cheese mixture over pasta and spinach; mix gently. Spoon onto a platter; scatter tomatoes over top. Season to taste with salt and pepper.

makes 4 servings

per serving: 537 calories, 30 g protein, 70 g carbohydrates, 17 g total fat, 107 mg cholesterol, 617 mg sodium

sautéed mizuna & shells

preparation time: about 25 minutes

1 pound mizuna, rinsed and drained

12 ounces medium-size dried pasta shells

2 tablespoons olive oil

1/4 teaspoon crushed red pepper flakes

1/2 cup grated Parmesan cheese

A feathery-leaved member of the mustard family, mildly tart mizuna is becoming increasingly available in well-stocked supermarkets and gourmet stores.

1. Trim off and discard bare stem ends and yellow or bruised leaves from mizuna; then chop leaves coarsely and set aside.

2. In a 5- to 6-quart pan, cook pasta in 3 quarts boiling water just until tender to bite (10 to 12 minutes); or cook according to package directions. When pasta is almost done, heat oil in a 4- to 5-quart pan over high heat. Add mizuna and stir until leaves are wilted (2 to 4 minutes).

3. Drain pasta and place in a warm serving bowl. Add mizuna; mix lightly, using 2 forks. Sprinkle with red pepper flakes and cheese; mix again.

makes 4 servings

per serving: 449 calories, 18 g protein, 69 g carbohydrates, 11 g total fat, 8 mg cholesterol, 219 mg sodium

farfalle with chard, garlic, and ricotta

preparation time: about 25 minutes

1 bunch chard, rinsed and drained

10 ounces dried farfalle (pasta bow ties)

2 tablespoons olive oil

1 medium-size onion, finely chopped

4 cloves garlic, minced or pressed

1 1/2 cups part-skim ricotta cheese, at room temperature

Salt and coarsely ground pepper

Grated Parmesan cheese (optional)

1. Trim off and discard ends of chard stems; then cut off remainder of stems at base or each leaf. Thinly slice stems and leaves crosswise, keeping them in separate piles. Set aside.

2. In a 5- to 6-quart pan, cook pasta in 3 quarts boiling water just until tender to bite (8 to 10 minutes); or cook according to package directions.

3. Meanwhile, heat oil in a wide (at least 12-inch) frying pan over medium-high heat. Add onion and chard stems; cook, stirring often, until onion is soft but not browned (3 to 5 minutes). Add garlic and chard leaves and cook, stirring often, until leaves are bright green (about 3 more minutes). Add 3/4 cup water and bring to a boil. Remove from heat and blend in ricotta cheese; season to taste with salt, pepper, and nutmeg.

4. Drain pasta well and place in a warm wide serving bowl. Ricotta mixture; mix lightly but thoroughly, using 2 forks to combine. If desired, serve with Parmesan cheese to add to taste.

makes 4 servings

per serving: 495 calories, 23 g protein, 67 g carbohydrates, 15 g total fat, 29 mg cholesterol, 400 mg sodium

pasta with artichokes & anchovies

preparation time: about 25 minutes

8 ounces dried linguine

1 jar (about 6 oz.) marinated artichoke hearts

2 cloves garlic, minced or pressed

1 tablespoon anchovy paste

1 can (about 2 1/4 oz.) sliced ripe olives, drained

1/2 cup chopped parsley

1/4 cup grated Parmesan cheese

Parsley sprigs

Pepper

1. In a 4- to 5-quart pan, cook linguine in about 8 cups boiling water until just tender to bite (8 to 10 minutes); or cook according to package directions. Drain well, transfer to a warm wide bowl, and keep warm.

2. While pasta is cooking, carefully drain marinade from artichokes into a wide nonstick frying pan or wok. Cut artichokes into bite-size pieces and set aside. Heat marinade over medium heat; add garlic and stir-fry until pale gold (about 3 minutes). Add anchovy paste, olives, and artichokes; stir-fry until heated through (about 2 minutes).

3. Pour artichoke mixture over pasta. Add chopped parsley and cheese; mix gently but thoroughly. Garnish with parsley sprigs; season to taste with pepper.

makes 4 to 6 servings

per serving: 245 calories, 10 g protein, 38 g carbohydrates, 6 g total fat, 5 mg cholesterol, 499 mg sodium

vermicelli with turkey

preparation time: about 30 minutes

8 ounces dried vermicelli

1/3 cup sun-dried tomatoes packed in oil, drained (reserve oil) and slivered

2 cloves garlic, minced or pressed

1 medium-size onion, chopped

1 large yellow or red bell pepper, chopped

3 medium-size zucchini, thinly sliced

1 cup fat-free reduced-sodium chicken broth

2 cups shredded cooked turkey breast

1/2 cup chopped fresh basil
  or 3 tablespoons dried basil

Freshly grated Parmesan cheese

1 Bring 8 cups water to a boil in a 4- to 5-quart pan over medium-high heat. Stir in pasta and cook just until tender to bite (8 to 10 minutes); or cook according to package directions.

2 Meanwhile, heat 1 tablespoon of the reserved oil from tomatoes in a wide nonstick frying pan over medium-high heat. Add tomatoes, garlic, onion, bell pepper, and zucchini. Cook, stirring often, until vegetables begin to brown (about 8 minutes).

3 Pour broth over vegetables and bring to a boil. Drain pasta well and add to vegetables with turkey and basil. Lift with 2 forks to mix. Transfer to a platter. Offer cheese to add to taste.

makes 4 servings

per serving: 500 calories, 33 g protein, 59 g carbohydrates, 16 g total fat, 59 mg cholesterol, 85 mg sodium

penne with turkey sausage

preparation time: about 35 minutes

12 ounces spinach, coarse stems removed, rinsed and drained

1 large red or yellow bell pepper, seeded

3 green onions

8 ounces dried penne

8 to 12 ounces mild or hot turkey Italian sausages, casings removed

1/2 cup balsamic vinegar (or 1/2 cup red wine vinegar and 5 teaspoons sugar)

1/2 to 3/4 teaspoon fennel seeds

Salt and pepper

1 Tear spinach into pieces. Cut bell pepper lengthwise into thin strips. Cut onions into 3-inch lengths and sliver lengthwise. Place vegetables in a large serving bowl and set aside.

2 Bring 8 cups water to a boil in a 4- to 5-quart pan over medium-high heat. Stir in pasta and cook just until tender to bite (8 to 10 minutes); or cook according to package directions. Drain well and keep warm.

3 Chop or crumble sausages. Cook in a wide nonstick frying pan or wok over medium-high heat, stirring often, until browned (about 10 minutes). Add vinegar and fennel seeds, stirring to loosen browned bits.

4 Add pasta to vegetables and immediately pour on sausage mixture; toss gently but well until spinach is slightly wilted. Serve immediately. Offer salt and pepper to add to taste.

makes 6 servings

per serving: 238 calories, 15 g protein, 32 g carbohydrates, 6 g total fat, 36 mg cholesterol, 327 mg sodium

fresh vegetables with fettuccine

preparation time: about 45 minutes

1 tablespoon olive oil

1 large onion, chopped

3 cloves garlic, minced or pressed

³/₄ pound mushrooms, thinly sliced

3 pounds pear-shaped (Roma-type) tomatoes, thinly sliced

2 tablespoons chopped fresh basil leaves

1 pound dry eggless fettuccine or linguine

¹/₂ pound carrots, thinly sliced

³/₄ pound *each* crookneck squash and zucchini, thinly sliced

¹/₄ cup *each* grated Parmesan cheese and thin strips of lean prosciutto

1. Heat oil in a 4- to 5-quart pan over medium-high heat. Add onion and cook, stirring occasionally, until soft (about 7 minutes). Add garlic and mushrooms; cook, stirring, until all liquid has evaporated (about 5 minutes). Add tomatoes and basil; continue to cook until mixture is thickened (about 10 more minutes), stirring occasionally.

2. Meanwhile, following package directions, cook fettuccine in boiling water until barely tender to bite; drain well. Place in a large, shallow serving bowl and keep warm.

3. Add carrots to sauce and cook for 5 minutes. Add crookneck squash and zucchini; continue to cook until vegetables are barely tender to bite (about 3 more minutes).

4. Spoon sauce over pasta and top with cheese and prosciutto.

makes 8 servings

per serving: 320 calories , 13 g protein, 60 g carbohydrates, 4 g total fat, 4 mg cholesterol, 122 mg sodium

korean noodles with hot sauce

preparation time: about 20 minutes

1 tablespoon Asian sesame oil

3 tablespoons distilled white vinegar

1 to 2 tablespoons hot bean paste

2 tablespoons soy sauce

3 tablespoons sliced green onion (including tops)

1 clove garlic, minced

1 teaspoon *each* sugar and pepper

2 teaspoons minced fresh ginger

2 tablespoons sesame seeds

12 ounces dry buckwheat noodles

1 medium-size cucumber, thinly sliced

1. In a bowl, combine sesame oil, vinegar, bean paste, soy, onions, garlic, sugar, pepper, and ginger. Set aside. Toast sesame seeds in a small frying pan over medium heat until golden (about 3 minutes), shaking pan frequently. Set aside.

2. Following package directions, cook noodles in boiling water until barely tender to bite. Drain; return to pan and add vinegar mixture and sesame seeds. Mix well. Garnish with cucumber.

makes 4 to 6 servings

per serving: 265 calories, 9 g protein, 47 g carbohydrates, 5 g total fat, 0 mg cholesterol, 367 mg sodium

asian pasta primavera

preparation time: about 40 minutes, plus 30 minutes to soak mushrooms

2 tablespoons sesame seeds

8 large dried or fresh shiitake mushrooms

¹/₂ pound *each* asparagus and bok choy

1 can (15 oz.) miniature corn, drained

1 pound dry whole wheat spaghetti

1 tablespoon salad oil

2 cloves garlic, minced or pressed

1 tablespoon very finely chopped fresh ginger

¹/₂ pound Chinese pea pods (also called snow or sugar peas) or sugar snap peas, ends and strings removed

1 can (about 8 oz.) sliced water chestnuts, drained

¹/₄ cup dry sherry

1 cup low-sodium chicken broth

2 tablespoons reduced-sodium soy sauce

1 teaspoon *each* sugar and white wine vinegar

1. Toast sesame seeds in a small frying pan over medium heat until golden (about 3 minutes), shaking pan frequently. Pour out of pan and set aside.

2. If using dried mushrooms, soak in warm water to cover for 30 minutes, then drain. Cut off and discard stems; squeeze caps dry and thinly slice. Or trim any tough stems from fresh mushrooms; thinly slice caps.

3. Snap off and discard tough ends of asparagus. Cut asparagus spears, bok choy stems and leaves, and corn into ¹/₂-inch slanting slices. Set aside.

4. Following package directions, cook spaghetti in boiling water until barely tender to bite; drain well. Place in a large, shallow serving bowl and keep warm.

5. Heat oil in a 12- to 14-inch frying pan over high heat. Add garlic and ginger and cook, stirring, until lightly browned (about 30 seconds). Add mushrooms, asparagus, bok choy, corn, pea pods, water chestnuts, and sherry. Cover and cook, stirring often, until vegetables are tender-crisp to bite (about 2 minutes). Spoon vegetables over noodles.

6. Add broth, soy, sugar, and vinegar to wok; bring to a boil, stirring. Pour over noodles and vegetables. Sprinkle with sesame seeds, then mix lightly. Serve immediately.

makes 8 servings

per serving: 304 calories, 14 g protein, 55 g carbohydrates, 4 g total fat, 0 mg cholesterol, 186 mg sodium

MUSHROOMS FROM HEAVEN: To experience a true vegetable delicacy that will be a delightful addition to your pasta, look for fresh porcini mushrooms in farmers' markets during the fall. These meaty fungi, with their dark brown caps and bulbous stems, are superb strewn into pasta and risotto. Also try them thickly sliced with olive oil and garlic, and grilled. To store fresh porcini, wrap them in paper towels, place them in a paper bag, and refrigerate for up to 2 days; gently wipe clean before using.

capellini with roasted tomatoes & white beans

preparation time: about 15 minutes
cooking time: about 1 ¼ hours

1 medium-size red onion, cut into ³/₄-inch chunks

1 tablespoon olive oil

6 tablespoons balsamic vinegar

14 medium-size pear-shaped (Roma-type) tomatoes, halved lengthwise

Salt

8 ounces dried capellini

2 cans (about 15 oz. *each*) cannnellini (white kidney beans)

3 tablespoons chopped fresh thyme or 1 tablespoon dried thyme

3 tablespoons chopped fresh basil or 1 tablespoon dried basil

Thyme sprigs

1 Mix onion, l teaspoon of the oil, and 2 tablespoons of the vinegar in a lightly oiled square 8-inch baking pan. Arrange tomatoes, cut sides up, in a lightly oiled 9-by 13-inch baking pan; rub with remaining 2 teaspoons oil and season to taste with salt.

2 Bake onion and tomatoes in a 475° oven, switching pan positions halfway through baking, until edges are well browned (40 to 50 minutes for onion, about 1 hour and 10 minutes for tomatoes); if drippings begin to burn, add 4 to 6 tablespoons water to each pan, stirring to loosen browned bits. Meanwhile, bring 8 cups water to a boil in a 4- to 5-quart pan over medium-high heat. Stir in pasta and cook just until tender to bite (about 4 minutes), or cook according to package directions.

3 Drain pasta well and keep warm. Pour beans and their liquid into pan. Add chopped thyme (or dried thyme and dried basil, if used). Bring to a boil; reduce heat and simmer, stirring often, for 3 minutes. Add pasta; lift with 2 forks to mix. Remove from heat; keep warm.

4 Chop 10 of the tomato halves. Add to pasta with chopped basil (if used), onion, and remaining ¼ cup vinegar. Transfer pasta to a wide, shallow serving bowl. Arrange remaining tomato halves around edge. Garnish with thyme sprigs.

makes 4 to 6 servings

per serving: 401 calories, 17 g protein, 73 g carbohydrates, 6 g total fat, 0 mg cholesterol, 616 mg sodium

linguini with yellow tomatoes

preparation time: about 30 minutes

1 pound dried linguine

About 2 tablespoons hot chili oil

1 clove garlic, minced or pressed

1 large onion, chopped

6 cups yellow or red cherry or other tiny tomatoes (or use some of each color), cut into halves

2 cups firmly packed fresh basil leaves

Basil sprigs (optional)

Grated Parmesan cheese

Salt

1 In a 6- to 8-quart pan, cook linguine in 4 quarts boiling water until just tender to bite (8 to 10 minutes); or cook according to package directions. Drain well, transfer to a wide bowl, and keep warm.

2 While pasta is cooking, heat 2 tablespoons of the chili oil in a wide non-stick frying pan or wok over medium-high heat. When oil is hot, add garlic and onion; stir-fry until onion is soft (about 5 minutes). Add tomatoes and basil leaves; stir gently until tomatoes are heated through (about 2 minutes).

3 Pour hot tomato mixture over pasta. Garnish with basil sprigs, if desired. Offer cheese to add to taste; season to taste with more chili oil and salt.

makes 6 to 8 servings

per serving: 322 calories, 10 g protein, 59 g carbohydrates, 5 g total fat, 0 mg cholesterol, 18 mg sodium

thai tofu & tagliatelle

preparation time: 35 to 40 minutes

1 cup vegetable broth

1 cup sugar

¼ cup reduced-sodium soy sauce

2 tablespoons cider vinegar

1 tablespoon cornstarch

2 teaspoons paprika

1 teaspoon crushed red pepper flakes

1 teaspoon vegetable oil

⅓ cup minced garlic

8 to 10 ounces dried tagliatelle or fettuccine

1 pound regular tofu, rinsed and drained, cut into ½-inch cubes

1 large red bell pepper, cut into ½-inch pieces

1 package (about 10 oz.) frozen tiny peas, thawed

1. Combine broth, sugar, soy sauce, vinegar, cornstarch, paprika, and red pepper flakes in a small bowl; mix until well blended. Set aside.

2. Heat oil in a wide nonstick frying pan over medium-high heat. Add garlic and cook, stirring often, until tinged with gold (about 4 minutes; do not scorch); if pan appears dry, stir in water, 1 tablespoon at a time.

3. Add broth mixture. Cook, stirring often, until sauce comes to a boil. Continue to cook until reduced to about 1¼ cups (10 to 15 minutes). Meanwhile, bring 12 cups water to a boil in a 5- to 6-quart pan over medium-high heat. Stir in pasta and cook just until tender to bite (8 to 10 minutes); or cook according to package directions. Drain well and transfer to a wide, shallow serving bowl.

4. Combine tofu, bell pepper, peas, and half the sauce in a large bowl. Mix well but gently. Spoon over pasta. Offer remaining sauce to add to taste.

makes 4 servings

per serving: 634 calories, 23 g protein, 121 g carbohydrates, 8 g total fat, 0 mg cholesterol, 987 mg sodium

farfalle with fresh tomatoes & basil

preparation time: about 20 minutes

12 ounces farfalle or other dry pasta shape

1 tablespoon olive oil

2 cloves garlic, minced or pressed

1 pound ripe pear-shaped tomatoes, coarsely chopped

1 cup tightly packed fresh basil leaves, torn into pieces

Coarsely ground pepper

Grated Parmesan cheese

1. In an 8- to 10-quart pan, cook pasta in 6 quarts boiling water until al dente (7 to 9 minutes or according to package directions).

2. Meanwhile, heat oil in a wide frying pan over medium heat. Add garlic and cook, stirring, for 1 minute. Add tomatoes and cook, stirring, just until tomatoes begin to soften (about 3 minutes). Remove from heat.

3. Drain pasta and place in a large, warm bowl or platter. Add tomato mixture and basil; toss well. Season to taste with pepper and offer with Parmesan.

makes 4 servings

per serving: 382 calories, 13 g protein, 72 g carbohydrates, 5 g total fat, 0 mg cholesterol, 16 mg sodium

peanut pasta & tofu

preparation time: about 40 minutes

1/4 cup seasoned rice vinegar (or 1/4 cup distilled white vinegar plus 2 teaspoons sugar)

3 tablespoons Asian sesame oil

1 tablespoon reduced-sodium soy sauce

1 teaspoon sugar

1 package (about 14 oz.) regular tofu, rinsed, drained, and cut into 1/2-inch cubes

12 ounces dried penne

2 cups Chinese pea pods (also called snow or sugar peas), ends and strings removed

2 cloves garlic, minced

1/2 cup plum jam

1/4 cup crunchy peanut butter

1/8 teaspoon ground ginger

1/3 cup cilantro leaves

1/4 cup sliced green onions

Cilantro sprigs

Crushed red pepper flakes

1. In a shallow bowl, beat vinegar, 1 tablespoon of the oil, soy sauce, and sugar until blended. Add tofu and mix gently. Set aside; stir occasionally.

2. In a 5- to 6-quart pan, bring about 3 quarts water to a boil over medium high heat; stir in pasta and cook until almost tender to bite, 7 to 9 minutes. (Or cook pasta according to package directions, cooking for a little less than the recommended time.) Add pea pods to boiling water with pasta and cook for 1 more minute. Drain pasta mixture, rinse with hot water, and drain well again; keep warm.

3. With a slotted spoon, transfer tofu to a large, shallow serving bowl; reserve marinade from tofu.

4. In pan used to cook pasta, heat remaining 2 tablespoons oil over medium heat. Add garlic and cook, stirring, just until fragrant (about 30 seconds; do not scorch). Add jam, peanut butter, marinade from tofu, and ginger. Cook, whisking, just until sauce is smooth and well blended.

5. Remove pan from heat and add pasta mixture, cilantro leaves, and onions. Mix gently but thoroughly. Transfer pasta to bowl with tofu and mix very gently. Garnish with cilantro sprigs. Serve at once; season to taste with red pepper flakes.

makes 4 servings

per serving: 714 calories, 25 g protein, 103 g carbohydrates, 25 g total fat, 0 mg cholesterol, 558 mg sodium

fettuccine cambozola

preparation time: about 20 minutes

1 package fresh fettuccine

1 package (about 10 oz.) frozen peas

1 cup diced cambozola or Gorgonzola cheese

Freshly ground pepper

1. Bring 3 quarts water to a boil in a 5- to 6-quart pan. Add pasta and cook just until tender to bite (3 to 4 minutes); or cook according to package directions. Stir in peas. Drain well.

2. Return pasta and peas to pan over low heat. Add cheese and 2 tablespoons hot water. Mix lightly until pasta is well coated with melted cheese (2 to 3 minutes).

3. Season to taste with pepper.

makes 2 to 4 servings

per serving: 492 calories, 23 g protein, 56 g carbohydrates, 18 g total fat, 233 mg cholesterol, 918 mg sodium

stuffed shells with roasted red pepper sauce

preparation time: about 20 minutes
cooking time: about 1 hour

Roasted Red Pepper Sauce (recipe below)

1 to 2 tablespoons pine nuts

20 jumbo shell-shaped pasta

1 can (about 15 oz.) garbanzo beans

¼ cup lightly packed fresh basil

2 tablespoons chopped parsley

2 tablespoons lemon juice

2 teaspoons Asian sesame oil

2 cloves garlic

¼ teaspoon ground cumin

Salt and pepper

Parsley sprigs

1 Prepare Roasted Red Pepper Sauce; set aside. Toast pine nuts in a small frying pan over medium heat, shaking pan often, until golden (about 3 minutes). Remove from pan and set aside.

2 Bring 12 cups water to a boil in a 5- to 6-quart pan over medium high heat. Stir in pasta and cook just until almost tender (about 8 minutes; do not overcook).

3 Meanwhile, drain beans, reserving liquid. Combine beans, basil, chopped parsley, lemon juice, oil, garlic and cumin in a blender or food processor. Whirl, adding reserved liquid as necessary, until smooth but thick. Season to taste with salt and pepper.

4 Drain pasta, rinse with cold water; and drain well. Spoon half the red pepper sauce into a shallow 2- to 2½-quart casserole Fill shells with bean mixture and arrange, filled, sides up, in sauce. Top with remaining sauce. Cover tightly and bake in a 350° oven until hot (about 40 minutes). Sprinkle with nuts. Garnish with parsley sprigs

makes 4 servings

per serving: 467 calories, 17 g protein, 80 g carbohydrates, 9 g total fat, 4 mg cholesterol, 424 mg sodium

roasted red pepper sauce

preparation time: about 30 minutes

Roasted Red Bell Peppers (directions follow)

1 teaspoon olive oil

1 large onion, chopped

3 cloves garlic, minced or pressed

2 tablespoons dry sherry (or to taste)

1 tablespoon white wine vinegar (or to taste)

⅛ teaspoon ground white pepper

¼ cup freshly grated

Parmesan cheese

Salt

1 Prepare Roasted Red Bell Peppers. Set aside with any drippings in a blender or food processor.

2 Heat oil in a wide nonstick frying pan over medium-high heat. Add onion and garlic. Cook, stirring often, until onion is soft (about 5 minutes); if pan appears dry or onion mixture sticks to pan bottom, add water, 1 tablespoon at a time.

3 Transfer onion mixture to blender with peppers. Whirl until smooth. Add sherry, vinegar, and pepper. Whirl until of desired consistency. (At this point, you may cover and refrigerate for up to 2 days; reheat before continuing.)

4 Add cheese. Season to taste with salt.

makes about 3 cups

ROASTED RED BELL PEPPERS

Cut 4 large red bell peppers in half lengthwise. Place, cut sides down, in a 10- by 15-inch baking pan. Broil 4 to 6 inches below heat, turning as needed, until charred all over (about 8 minutes). Cover with foil and let cool in pan. Pull off and discard skins, stems, and seeds. Cut into chunks.

per serving: 40 calories, 1 g protein, 6 g carbohydrates, 1 g total fat, 1 mg cholesterol, 33 mg sodium

fettuccine alfredo

preparation time: 40 minutes

2 cans (about 14 oz. *each*) artichoke hearts packed in water, drained and quartered

3 tablespoons chopped Italian or regular parsley

3 tablespoons thinly sliced green onions

12 ounces dried fettuccine

1 tablespoon butter or olive oil

3 cloves garlic, minced

1 tablespoon, all-purpose flour

1 1/2 cups low-fat (2%) milk

1 large package (about 8 oz.) nonfat cream cheese, cut into small chunks

1 1/2 cups (about 4 1/2 oz.) shredded Parmesan cheese

1/8 teaspoon ground nutmeg (optional)

Pepper

1. In a medium-size bowl, combine artichokes, parsley, and onions. Set aside.

2. In a 5- to 6-quart pan, bring about 3 quarts water to a boil over medium high heat; stir in pasta and cook until just tender to bite, 8 to 10 minutes. (Or cook pasta according to package directions.) Drain well, return to pan, and keep hot.

3. Melt butter in a wide nonstick frying pan over medium heat. Add garlic and cook, stirring, until fragrant (about 30 seconds: do not scorch). Whisk in flour until well blended, then gradually whisk in milk Cook, whisking constantly, until mixture boils and thickens slightly (about 5 minutes). Whisk in cream cheese, 1 cup of the Parmesan cheese, and nutmeg (if desired). Continue to cook, whisking constantly, until cheese is melted and evenly blended into sauce.

4. Working quickly, pour hot sauce over pasta and lift with 2 forks to mix. Spoon pasta into center of 4 shallow individual bowls. Then quickly arrange artichoke mixture around pasta. Sprinkle with remaining 1/2 cup Parmesan cheese, then with pepper. Serve immediately (sauce thickens rapidly and is absorbed quickly by pasta).

makes 4 servings

per serving: 641 calories, 39 g protein, 82 g carbohydrates, 17 g total fat, 126 mg cholesterol, 924 mg sodium

baked penne with radicchio

preparation time: 40 to 45 minutes

8 ounces dry penne or mostaccioli

1 tablespoon olive oil

8 ounces mushrooms, sliced

2 cloves garlic, minced or pressed

1 teaspoon dry sage

4 cups lightly packed shredded radicchio

1/4 cup grated Parmesan cheese

1/4 cup crumbled Gorgonzola or other blue veined cheese

Freshly ground pepper

1 cup evaporated skim milk

1. In a 5- to 6-quart pan, cook penne in 3 quarts boiling water just until almost tender to bite (10 to 12 minutes); or cook a little less than time specified in package directions.

2. Meanwhile, heat oil in a wide nonstick frying pan over medium heat; add mushrooms, garlic, and sage. Cook, stirring often, until mushrooms are soft and liquid has evaporated (about 10 minutes). Stir in radicchio, then remove pan from heat.

3. Drain pasta well; add to mushroom mixture along with Parmesan and Gorgonzola cheeses, then mix lightly. Season to taste with pepper. Transfer to a greased 2- to 2½-quart casserole; drizzle evenly with milk. Cover and bake in a 450° oven until bubbly and heated through (15 to 20 minutes).

makes 4 servings

per serving: 366 calories, 17 g protein, 55 g carbohydrates, 9 g total fat, 14 mg cholesterol, 263 mg sodium

orecchiette with lentils & goat cheese

preparation time: about 45 minutes

2 cups vegetable broth

6 ounces lentils, rinsed and drained

1 tablespoon chopped fresh thyme
  or 1 teaspoon dried thyme

8 ounces dried orecchiette
  or other medium-size pasta shape

1/3 cup white wine vinegar

3 tablespoons chopped parsley

2 tablespoons olive oil

1 teaspoon honey, or to taste

1 clove garlic, minced or pressed

1/2 cup crumbled goat or feta cheese

Thyme sprigs

Salt and pepper

1. Bring broth to a boil in a 1½- to 2-quart pan over high heat. Add lentils and chopped thyme; reduce heat, cover, and simmer until lentils are tender to bite (20 to 30 minutes).

2. Meanwhile, bring 8 cups water to a boil in a 4- to 5-quart pan over medium-high heat. Stir in pasta and cook just until tender to bite (8 to 10 minutes); or cook according to package directions. Drain pasta and, if necessary, lentils well. Transfer pasta and lentils to a large serving bowl; keep warm.

3. Combine vinegar, parsley, oil, honey, and garlic in a small bowl. Beat until blended. Add to pasta mixture and mix thoroughly but gently. Sprinkle with cheese. Garnish with thyme sprigs. Offer salt and pepper to add to taste.

makes 4 servings

per serving: 514 calories, 25 g protein, 75 g carbohydrates, 14 g total fat, 13 mg cholesterol, 648 mg sodium

spaghetti with beans and spaghetti squash

preparation time: about 15 minutes
cooking time: about 1 3/4 hours

1 spaghetti squash

1 1/2 cups vegetable broth

1 package (about 10 oz.) frozen baby lima beans

2 tablespoons fresh thyme
  or 2 teaspoons dried thyme

1 1/2 teaspoons grated lemon peel

8 cups lightly packed spinach leaves,
  cut into narrow strips

12 ounces dried spaghetti

Salt and pepper

1. Pierce squash shell in several places. Place in a shallow pan slightly larger than squash. Bake in a 350° oven until shell gives readily when pressed (1 ¼ to 1 ½ hours).

2. Halve squash lengthwise; remove seeds. Scrape squash from shell, using a fork to loosen strands, and place in a 3- to 4-quart pan. Add broth, beans, thyme, and lemon peel. Bring to a boil over high heat; reduce heat, cover, and simmer, stirring often, just until beans are tender to bite (about 5 minutes). Add spinach. Cover and cook until spinach is wilted (1 to 2 more minutes). Remove from heat and keep warm.

3. Bring 12 cups water to a boil in a 5- to 6-quart pan over medium-high heat. Stir in pasta and cook just until tender to bite (8 to 10 minutes); or cook according to package directions. Drain well; return to pan. Add squash mixture and lift with 2 forks to mix. Transfer to a serving bowl. Offer salt and pepper to add to taste

makes 8 servings

per serving: 259 calories, 11 g protein, 51 g carbohydrates, 2 g total fat, 0 mg cholesterol, 301 mg sodium

oven-baked mediterreanean orzo

preparation time: about 1 hour

2 large cans (about 28 oz.) tomatoes

About 2 cups vegetable broth

1 teaspoon olive oil

2 large onion, cut into very thin slivers

1 can (about 15 oz.) *each* black beans and
   cannellini (white kidney beans, drained
   and rinsed well)

1 package (about 9 oz.) frozen artichoke hearts,
   (thawed and drained)

$^1/_2$ cup dried apricots, cut into halves

$^1/_3$ cup raisins

About 1 tablespoon drained capers (or to taste)

4 teaspoons chopped fresh basil
   or 1 $^1/_2$ teaspoons dried basil

$^1/_2$ teaspoon fennel seeds, crushed

1 $^1/_2$ cups dried orzo or other rice-shaped pasta

$^1/_2$ cup crumbled feta cheese

Pepper

1. Break up tomatoes with a spoon and drain liquid into a 4-cup measure; set tomatoes aside. Add enough of the broth to tomato liquid to make 3 cups; set aside.

2. Place oil and onion in an oval 3- to 3½-quart casserole, about 9 by 13 inches and at least 2½ inches deep. Bake in a 450° oven until onion is soft and tinged with brown (about 10 minutes). During baking, stir occasionally to loosen browned bits from casserole bottom; add water, 1 tablespoon at a time, if casserole appears dry.

3. Remove casserole from oven and carefully add tomatoes, broth mixture, black beans, cannellini, artichokes, apricots, raisins, capers, basil, and fennel seeds. Stir to loosen any browned bits from casserole. Return to oven and continue to bake until mixture comes to a rolling boil (about 20 minutes).

4. Remove casserole from oven and carefully stir in pasta, scraping casserole bottom to loosen any browned bits. Cover tightly, return to oven, and bake for 10 more minutes; then stir pasta mixture well, scraping casserole bottom. Cover tightly again and continue to bake until pasta is just tender to bite and almost all liquid has been absorbed (about 10 more minutes). Sprinkle with cheese, cover and let stand for about 5 minutes before serving. Season to taste with pepper.

makes 6 to 8 servings

per serving: 358 calories, 35 g protein, 66 g carbohydrates, 5 g total fat, 9 mg cholesterol, 847 mg sodium

STORE BREAD IN THE FREEZER: You'll always have fresh bread if you keep a loaf in the freezer. Bread kept at room temperature must be used quickly, and refrigerated bread can dry out rapidly. To thaw frozen bread in a hurry, spread out slices in a single layer and let stand for 10 minutes. If slices are to be toasted, put them right into the toaster.

bucatini & black beans

preparation time: about 35 minutes

10 ounces dried bucatini, perciatelli, or spaghetti

$^2/_3$ cup seasoned rice vinegar (or $^2/_3$ cup distilled white vinegar and 2 tablespoons sugar)

2 tablespoons honey

1 tablespoon olive oil

$^1/_2$ teaspoon chili oil

2 cans (about 15 oz. *each*) black beans, drained and rinsed

4 large pear-shaped tomatoes (about 12 oz. *total*), diced

$^1/_3$ cup finely chopped parsley

$^1/_4$ cup thinly sliced green onions

$^3/_4$ cup crumbled feta cheese

Parsley sprigs

1. Bring 12 cups water to a boil in a 5- to 6-quart pan over medium-high heat. Stir in pasta and cook just until tender to bite (10 to 12 minutes); or cook according to package directions. Drain well and keep warm.

2. Combine vinegar, honey, olive oil, and chili oil in pan. Bring just to a boil over medium-high heat. Add pasta, beans, and tomatoes. Cook, stirring, until hot. Remove from heat; stir in chopped parsley and onions.

3. Spoon pasta mixture into bowls. Sprinkle with cheese. Garnish with parsley sprigs.

makes 4 servings

per serving: 564 calories, 21 g protein, 96 g carbohydrates, 11 g total fat, 23 mg cholesterol, 1,095 mg sodium

pasta with shrimp & shiitakes

preparation time: about 35 minutes

2 cups dried shiitake mushrooms

8 ounces dried capellini

2 teaspoons Asian sesame oil

6 tablespoons oyster sauce or reduced-sodium soy sauce

1 tablespoon vegetable oil

12 ounces medium-size raw shrimp (31 to 35 per lb.), shelled and deveined

1 tablespoon finely chopped fresh ginger

3 green onions, thinly sliced

1. Place mushrooms in a medium-size bowl and add enough boiling water to cover, let stand until mushrooms are softened (about 10 minutes). Squeeze mushrooms dry. Cut off and discard stems. Slice caps into strips about $^1/_4$ inch thick.

2. In a 4- to 5-quart pan, bring about 8 cups water to a boil over medium-high heat; stir in pasta and cook until just tender to bite, about 3 minutes. (Or cook according to package directions.) Drain pasta, rinse with hot water, and drain well again. Then return to pan, add sesame oil and 3 tablespoons of the oyster sauce; lift with 2 forks to mix well. Keep pasta mixture warm.

3. Heat vegetable oil in a wide nonstick frying pan over medium-high heat. Add mushrooms, shrimp, and ginger. Cook, stirring often, until shrimp are just opaque in center, cut to test (about 5 minutes). Add onions and remaining 3 tablespoons oyster sauce; mix thoroughly. Pour noodles into a wide bowl; pour shrimp mixture over noodles.

makes 4 servings

per serving: 409 calories, 25 g protein, 64 g carbohydrates, 8 g total fat, 105 mg cholesterol, 1,181 mg sodium

ziti with turkey, feta & sun-dried tomatoes

preparation time: about 30 minutes

2 to 4 tablespoons sun-dried tomatoes in olive oil

1/2 cup fat-free reduced-sodium chicken broth

2 tablespoons dry white wine

1 teaspoon cornstarch

1 small onion

8 ounces dried ziti or penne

2 turkey breast tenderloins (about 1 lb. *total*), cut into 1/2-inch pieces

1 1/2 teaspoons chopped fresh oregano or 1/2 teaspoon dried oregano

1 large tomato, chopped and drained well

2 tablespoons drained capers

1/2 cup crumbled feta cheese

Oregano sprigs

1 Drain sun-dried tomatoes well (reserve oil) and pat dry with paper towels. Then chop tomatoes and set aside.

2 To prepare sauce, in a small bowl, stir together broth, wine, and cornstarch until blended; set aside.

3 Chop onion and set aside.

4 In a 4- to 5-quart pan, cook pasta in about 8 cups boiling water until just tender to bite (8 to 10 minutes). Drain pasta well and transfer to a warm large bowl; keep warm.

5 While pasta is cooking, measure 2 teaspoons of the oil from sun-dried tomatoes. Heat oil in a wide nonstick frying pan or wok over medium-high heat. When oil is hot, add turkey and chopped oregano. Stir-fry just until meat is no longer pink in center cut to test (2 to 3 minutes). Add water, 1 tablespoon at a time, if pan appears to be dry. Remove turkey with a slotted spoon; transfer to bowl with pasta and keep warm.

6 Add sun-dried tomatoes and onion to pan; stir-fry until onion is soft (about 4 minutes). Add water if pan is dry.

7 Stir reserved sauce well and pour into pan. Cook, stirring, until sauce boils and thickens slightly (1 to 2 minutes). Remove from heat and stir in fresh tomato and capers. Spoon tomato mixture over pasta and turkey; mix gently but thoroughly.

8 Divide turkey mixture among 4 warm individual rimmed plates or shallow bowls. Sprinkle with cheese and garnish with oregano sprigs.

makes 4 servings

per serving: 489 calories, 39 g protein, 52 g carbohydrates, 13 g total fat, 83 mg cholesterol, 464 mg sodium

mixed herb pesto

preparation time: 15 minutes

2 cups lightly packed fresh basil leaves

1/2 cup thinly sliced green onions

1/3 cup lightly packed fresh oregano leaves

1/4 cup grated Parmesan cheese

1/4 cup red wine vinegar

2 tablespoons fresh rosemary leaves

2 tablespoons olive oil

1/4 to 1/2 teaspoon pepper

In a food processor or blender, whirl basil, onions, oregano, cheese, vinegar, rosemary, oil, and pepper until smoothly puréed.

makes about 1 cup

per tablespoon: 29 calories, 0.9 g protein, 2 g carbohydrates, 2 g total fat, 1 mg cholesterol, 25 mg sodium

linguine with lentils

preparation time: about 55 minutes

1 cup lentils

2 cups canned vegetable broth

1 teaspoon dried thyme

1/3 cup lemon juice

3 tablespoons chopped fresh basil

2 tablespoons olive oil

1 teaspoon honey (or to taste)

2 cloves garlic, minced

12 ounces dried Linguine

1 large tomato, chopped and drained

3/4 cup grated Parmesan cheese

1 Rinse and sort lentils, discarding any debris; drain lentils. In a 1 1/2- to 2-quart part, bring broth to a basil over high heat; add lentils and thyme. Reduce heat, cover, and simmer just until lentils are tender to bite (25 to 30 minutes). Drain and discard any remaining cooking liquid; keep lentils warm.

2 While lentils are cooking, combine lemon juice, chopped basil, oil, honey, and garlic in a small bowl; set aside. Also bring about 3 quarts water to a boil in a 5- to 6-quart pan over medium-high heat; stir in pasta and cook until just tender to bite, 8 to 10 minutes. (Or cook pasta according to package directions.)

3 Working quickly, drain pasta well and transfer to a large serving bowl. Add basil mixture, lentils, and tomato. Lift with 2 forks to mix. Sprinkle with cheese and serve immediately.

makes 6 servings

per serving: 426 calories, 23 g protein, 66 g carbohydrates, 9 g total fat, 8 mg cholesterol, 537 mg sodium

three-cheese lasagne with chard

preparation time: 20 minutes
cooking time: about 1 hour

12 ounces dry lasagne noodles

2 1/2 cups low-fat (2%) milk

1/4 cup cornstarch

1 1/2 teaspoons dried basil

1/2 teaspoon *each* dried rosemary and salt

1/4 teaspoon ground nutmeg

1 cup nonfat ricotta cheese

2 packages (about 10 oz. *each*) frozen chopped Swiss chard, thawed and squeezed dry

2 large ripe tomatoes, chopped

2 cups shredded mozzarella cheese

1/3 cup grated Parmesan cheese

1 In a 5- to 6-quart pan, bring about 3 quarts water to a boil over medium-high heat; stir in pasta and cook until just barely tender to bite, about 8 minutes. Drain pasta well and lay out flat; cover lightly.

2 In pasta-cooking pan, smoothly blend milk, cornstarch, basil, rosemary, salt, and nutmeg. Stir over medium-high heat until mixture boils and thickens slightly (about 5 minutes). Stir in ricotta cheese, chard, tomatoes, and half the mozzarella cheese. Gently stir in pasta.

3 Transfer mixture to a 9- by 13-inch baking pan; gently push pasta down to cover it with sauce. Sprinkle with remaining mozzarella cheese, then with Parmesan cheese. Bake in a 375° oven until lasagne is bubbly in center (about 40 minutes). Let stand for about 5 minutes before serving.

makes 8 servings

per serving: 362 calories, 22 g protein, 48 g carbohydrates, 10 g total fat, 33 mg cholesterol, 531 mg sodium

low-fat lo mein

preparation time: about 30 minutes

12 ounces fresh Chinese noodles or linguine

1 teaspoon Asian sesame oil

1 tablespoon vegetable oil

1 small onion, thinly sliced lengthwise

2 tablespoons oyster sauce

8 ounces ground turkey

1 pound napa cabbage, thinly sliced crosswise

4 ounces oyster mushrooms, thinly sliced

2 medium-size carrots, cut into matchstick strips

1/2 cup fat-free reduced-sodium chicken broth

2 tablespoons reduced-sodium soy sauce

1 In a 5- to 6-quart pan, cook noodles in about 3 quarts boiling water until just tender to bite (3 to 5 minutes); or cook according to package directions. Drain well, toss with sesame oil, and keep warm.

2 Heat vegetable oil in a wide nonstick frying pan or wok over medium-high heat. When oil is hot, add onion and oyster sauce; then crumble in turkey. Stir-fry until onion is soft and turkey is no longer pink (about 3 minutes). Add cabbage, mushrooms, carrots, and broth; cover and cook until carrots are just tender to bite (about 3 minutes). Uncover and continue to cook until liquid has evaporated (1 to 2 more minutes). Stir in soy sauce; add noodles and stir-fry until heated.

makes 6 servings

per serving: 295 calories, 16 g protein, 41 g carbohydrates, 7 g total fat, 69 mg cholesterol, 563 mg sodium

spinach pasta & scallops

preparation time: about 30 minutes

8 ounces dried spinach fettuccine or 1 package (9 oz.) fresh spinach fettuccine

2 tablespoons pine nuts

2 tablespoons olive oil

1 pound bay scallops, rinsed and patted dry

2 cloves garlic, minced or pressed

1 large tomato, seeded and chopped

1/4 cup dry white wine

1/4 cup chopped Italian parsley

Salt and freshly ground pepper

1 In a 5- to 6-quart pan, cook fettuccine in 3 quarts boiling water just until tender to bite (8 to 10 minutes for dry pasta, 3 to 4 minutes for fresh); or cook according to package directions. Drain well.

2 While pasta is cooking, toast pine nuts in a wide nonstick frying pan over medium-low heat until lightly browned (about 3 minutes), stirring often. Remove nuts from pan and set aside. Then heat oil in pan over medium-high heat. Add scallops and cook, turning often with a wide spatula, until opaque in center, cut to test (2 to 3 minutes). Lift from pan, place on a warm plate, and keep warm.

3 Add garlic to pan; cook, stirring, just until it begins to brown (1 to 2 minutes). Stir in tomato, then wine; bring to a full boil. Remove pan from heat and add pasta, scallops and any accumulated liquid, and parsley; mix lightly, using 2 spoons. Season to taste with salt and pepper. Sprinkle with pine nuts.

makes 4 servings

per serving: 425 calories, 29 g protein, 47 g carbohydrates, 13 g total fat, 91 mg cholesterol, 231 mg sodium

pasta with chicken & prosciutto

preparation time: about 25 minutes

¹/₂ cup fat-free reduced-sodium chicken broth or dry white wine

¹/₄ cup Dijon mustard

2 tablespoons lemon juice

1 teaspoon dried basil

8 ounces dried spinach spaghetti

2 teaspoons olive oil

4 green onions, thinly sliced

2 cloves garlic, minced or pressed

1 ounce prosciutto, cut into thin strips

1 pound skinless, boneless chicken breast, cut into ¹/₂- by 2-inch strips

1 In a small bowl, stir together broth, mustard, lemon juice, and basil. Set aside.

2 In a 4- to 5-quart pan, cook spaghetti in about 8 cups boiling water until just tender to bite (8 to 10 minutes); or cook according to package directions.

3 Meanwhile, heat oil in a wide nonstick frying pan or wok over medium heat. When oil is hot, add onions, garlic, and prosciutto; stir-fry until prosciutto is lightly browned (about 3 minutes). Increase heat to medium-high. Add chicken and stir-fry until no longer pink in center, cut to test (3 to 4 minutes). Add broth mixture to pan and bring to a boil. Remove from heat.

4 Drain pasta well and place in a warm wide bowl; spoon chicken mixture over pasta.

makes 4 servings

per serving: 399 calorie, 37 g protein, 45 g carbohydrates, 6 g total fat, 72 mg cholesterol, 670 mg sodium

fettuccine with shrimp & gorgonzola

preparation time: about 25 minutes

12 ounces dried spinach fettuccine or regular fettuccine

2 teaspoons butter or margarine

12 ounces mushrooms, sliced

³/₄ cup half-and-half

3 ounces Gorgonzola cheese, crumbled

³/₄ cup fat-free reduced-sodium chicken broth

8 ounces tiny cooked shrimp

2 tablespoons minced parsley

1 Bring 12 cups water to a boil in a 5- to 6-quart pan over medium-high heat. Stir in pasta and cook just until tender to bite (8 to 10 minutes); or cook according to package directions. Drain well and keep warm.

2 Melt butter in a wide nonstick frying pan over medium-high heat. Add mushrooms and cook, stirring often, until browned (about 8 minutes). Add half-and-half, cheese, and broth. Reduce heat to medium and cook, stirring, until cheese is melted (about 2 minutes); do not boil.

3 Add shrimp and pasta quickly. Lift with 2 forks until most of the liquid is absorbed. Transfer to a platter. Sprinkle with parsley.

makes 6 servings

per serving: 372 calories, 22 g protein, 44 g carbohydrates, 12 g total fat, 153 mg cholesterol, 366 mg sodium

farfalle with smoked salmon & vodka

preparation time: about 40 minutes

12 ounces dried farfalle

1 teaspoon olive oil

1 small shallot, thinly sliced

4 small pear-shaped (Roma-type) tomatoes, peeled, seeded, and chopped

2/3 cup half-and-half

3 tablespoons vodka

2 tablespoons chopped fresh dill or 1/2 teaspoon dried dill weed, or to taste

Pinch of ground nutmeg

4 to 6 ounces sliced smoked salmon or lox, cut into bite-size strips

Dill sprigs

Ground white pepper

1 Bring 12 cups water to a boil in a 5- to 6-quart pan over medium-high heat. Stir in pasta and cook just until tender to bite (8 to 10 minutes); or cook according to package directions. Drain well and keep warm.

2 Heat oil in a wide nonstick frying pan over medium-low heat. Add shallot and cook, stirring often, until soft but not browned (about 3 minutes). Stir in tomatoes; cover and simmer for 5 minutes. Add half-and-half, vodka, chopped dill, and nutmeg. Increase heat to medium-high and bring to a boil. Cook, stirring often, for 1 minute.

3 Add pasta and mix thoroughly but gently. Remove from heat and stir in salmon. Transfer to a serving platter. Garnish with dill sprigs. Offer white pepper to add to taste.

makes 5 servings

per serving: 385 calories, 15 g protein, 54 g carbohydrates, 10 g total fat, 28 mg cholesterol, 243 mg sodium

pasta with parsley-lemon pesto

preparation time: about 20 minutes

1 pound penne, rigatoni, or other dry pasta shape

1 large lemon

2 cups lightly packed chopped fresh parsley (preferably Italian)

2 cloves garlic

3 ounces grated Parmesan cheese

3 tablespoons extra-virgin olive oil

Coarsely ground pepper

1 In an 8- to 10-quart pan, cook pasta in 6 quarts boiling water until al dente (7 to 9 minutes or according to package directions).

2 Meanwhile, use a vegetable peeler to pare zest (colored part of peel) from lemon in large strips (reserve lemon for other uses). In a food processor, whirl lemon zest, parsley, garlic, and Parmesan until finely minced, scraping down sides of bowl as needed. (Or mince lemon zest, parsley, and garlic by hand; stir in cheese.)

3 Drain pasta and place in a large, warm bowl. Add parsley mixture and oil; toss well. Season to taste with pepper.

makes 4 to 6 servings

per serving: 487 calories, 18 g protein, 71 g carbohydrates, 14 g total fat,, 12 mg cholesterol, 289 mg sodium

rotini with scallops

preparation time: about 30 minutes

1 pound dried rotini or other corkscrew-shaped pasta

1 1/2 pounds bay scallops, rinsed and drained

1 teaspoon paprika

1/2 teaspoon dried basil

1/2 teaspoon dried thyme

1/2 teaspoon dry mustard

1/2 teaspoon ground white pepper

2 teaspoons vegetable oil

1 cup fat-free reduced-sodium chicken broth

1 1/2 tablespoons cornstarch blended with 1/3 cup water

1/2 cup reduced-fat or regular sour cream

1. Bring 16 cups water to a boil in a 6- to 8-quart pan over medium-high heat. Stir in pasta and cook just until tender to bite (8 to 10 minutes); or cook according to package directions.

2. Meanwhile, place scallops in a large bowl. Add paprika, basil, thyme, mustard, and white pepper. Mix until scallops are well coated.

3. Heat oil in a wide nonstick frying pan over medium-high heat. Add scallops and cook, stirring often, just until opaque in center; cut to test (about 3 minutes). Lift out and set aside, reserving juices in pan.

4. Drain pasta well. Transfer to a serving platter and keep warm.

5. Increase heat to high and cook reserved juices until reduced to about 1/4 cup. Add broth and bring to a boil. Stir cornstarch mixture well and add to broth. Bring to a boil again, stirring constantly. Remove from heat and stir in sour cream and scallops. Spoon over pasta.

makes 6 servings

per serving: 442 calories, 31 g protein, 63 g carbohydrates, 7 g total fat, 44 mg cholesterol, 218 mg sodium

linguini with red & green sauce

preparation time: about 1 hour

8 medium-size red bell peppers

1 pound dried linguine

1 cup thinly sliced green onions

1 can (about 35 oz.) garbanzo beans, drained

3/4 cup chopped fresh basil or 1/4 cup dried basil

1 1/2 tablespoons chopped fresh tarragon or 1 1/2 teaspoons dried tarragon

3 tablespoons capers, drained

Salt and pepper

1. Place bell peppers in a 10- by 15- inch baking pan. Broil about 3 inches below heat, turning as needed, until charred all over (about 15 minutes). Cover with foil and let cool in pan. Pull off and discard skins, stems, and seeds. Chop finely in a food processor or with a knife. Set aside.

2. Bring 16 cups water to a boil in a 6-to 8-quart pan over medium-high heat. Stir in pasta and cook just until tender to bite (8 to 10 minutes); or cook according to package instructions. Meanwhile, combine bell peppers, onions, beans, basil, tarragon, and capers in a 3- to 4- quart pan. Cook over medium-high heat, stirring often, until steaming (5 to 7 minutes).

3. Drain pasta well and transfer to a wide, shallow serving bowl. Add vegetable mixture and lift with 2 forks to mix. Offer salt and pepper to taste.

makes 8 servings

per serving: 295 calories, 11 g protein, 59 g carbohydrates, 12 g total fat, 0 mg cholesterol, 151 mg sodium

sicilian pasta timbale

preparation time: 20 minutes, plus 15 minutes for eggplant to stand
cooking time: about 1 hour

MARINARA SAUCE:

1 teaspoon olive oil

3 cloves garlic, minced or pressed

1 large can (about 28 oz.) tomato purée

**¼ cup chopped fresh basil
  or 2 tablespoons dried basil**

PASTA TIMBALE:

2 small eggplants

2 teaspoons salt

4 to 6 teaspoons olive oil

1 pound dried salad macaroni

2 cups shredded provolone cheese

½ cup grated Romano cheese

**About 3 teaspoon butter
  or margarine at room temperature**

2 tablespoons fine dry bread crumbs

Garnish

Basil sprigs

1. Heat the 1 teaspoon oil in a 3- to 4-quart pan over medium heat. Add garlic and cook, stirring, just until fragrant (about 30 seconds; do not scorch). Add tomato purée and chopped basil. Bring to a boil; then reduce heat and simmer, uncovered, stirring occasionally, until sauce is reduced to about 3 cups (about 20 minutes). Season to taste with salt; set aside.

2. While sauce is simmering, cut eggplants lengthwise into ¼-inch slices; sprinkle with the 2 teaspoons salt. Let stand for 15 minutes; then rinse well and pat dry. Coat 2 or 3 shallow 10- by 15-inch baking pans with oil, using 2 teaspoons oil per pan. Turn eggplant slices in oil to coat both sides; arrange in a single layer. Bake in a 425° oven until eggplant is browned and soft when pressed (about 25 minutes; remove pieces as they brown).

3. In a 6- to 8-quart pan, bring about 4 quarts water to a boil over medium-high heat; stir in pasta and cook until just barely tender to bite (6 to 8 minutes); or cook pasta according to package directions, cooking slightly less than time recommended. Drain pasta well and mix with provolone cheese, 2 cups of the marinara sauce, and 6 tablespoons of the Romano cheese.

4. Butter sides and bottom of a 9-inch cheesecake pan. Dust pan with bread crumbs. Arrange a third of the eggplant slices in pan, overlapping them to cover bottom of pan. Cover with half the pasta mixture. Add a layer of half the remaining eggplant, then evenly top with remaining pasta mixture. Top evenly with remaining eggplant. Press down gently to compact layers and to make timbale level. Sprinkle with remaining 2 tablespoons Romano cheese. (At this point, you may cover and refrigerate until next day.)

5. Bake, uncovered, in a 350° oven until hot in center, about 30 minutes. (If refrigerated, bake, covered, for 30 minutes; then uncover and continue to bake until hot in center, about 30 more minutes.) Let stand for about 5 minutes before serving.

6. Meanwhile, pour remaining marinara sauce into a 1- to 1½-quart pan, stir over medium heat until steaming. Transfer to a small pitcher or sauce boat. With a knife, cut around edge of timbale to release; remove pan rim. Garnish timbale with basil sprigs. Cut into wedges; serve with hot marinara sauce.

makes 6 to 8 servings

per serving: 503 calories, 22 g protein, 71 g carbohydrates, 15 g total fat, 30 mg cholesterol, 994 mg sodium

green & red lasagne

preparation time: about 35 minutes
cooking time: about 1 hour and 20 minutes

Tomato-Mushroom Sauce (recipe follows)

1 egg

1 egg white

1 package (about 10 oz.) frozen chopped spinach, thawed and squeezed dry

2 cups low-fat cottage cheese

⅓ cup grated Romano cheese

¼ teaspoon pepper

⅛ teaspoon ground nutmeg

8 ounces dry lasagne noodles

1½ cups shredded part-skim mozzarella cheese

1 Prepare Tomato-Mushroom Sauce. Meanwhile, in a medium-size bowl, beat egg and egg white to blend; then stir in spinach, cottage and Romano cheeses, pepper, and nutmeg.

2 Spread a fourth of the sauce in a 9- by 13-inch casserole; top with a third of the uncooked lasagne noodles. Spoon on a third of the spinach mixture.

3 Repeat layers of sauce, lasagne, and spinach mixture until all ingredients are used; end with sauce. Sprinkle with mozzarella cheese. Cover tightly with foil. (At this point, you may refrigerate until next day).

4 Bake, covered, in a 375° oven until lasagne noodles are tender to bite (about 1 hour; about 1½ hours if refrigerated). Let stand, covered, for about 10 minutes; then cut into squares to serve.

makes 6 to 8 servings

TOMATO-MUSHROOM SAUCE

Heat 1 teaspoon olive oil in a wide (at least 12-inch) nonstick frying pan over medium heat. Add 2 large onions, finely chopped; 1 large red bell pepper, seeded and finely chopped; 8 ounces mushrooms, thinly sliced; 3 cloves garlic, minced or pressed; 1 teaspoon dry oregano; and 2½ teaspoons dry basil. Cook, stirring often, until liquid has evaporated and onion is very soft (15 to 20 minutes). Stir in 1 large can (about 15 oz.) no-salt-added tomato sauce, 1 can (about 6 oz.) tomato paste, 1 tablespoon reduced-sodium soy sauce and ½ cup dry red wine. Cook, stirring, until sauce comes to a boil; use hot.

per serving: 365 calories, 25 g protein, 46 g carbohydrates, 8 g total fat, 51 mg cholesterol, 765 mg sodium

PASTA NUTRITION: Pasta is low in fat and sodium; it's a good source of complex carbohydrates, and enriched pastas provide B-vitamins and iron. The durum wheat from which most pasta is made is high in protein. Finally, pasta's calorie content is lower than you may have assumed—2 ounces of uncooked spaghetti or macaroni provide less than 210 calories.

tortellini with roasted eggplant, garlic and pepper

preparation time: about 45 minutes

2 large red bell peppers, roasted

Balsamic Vinegar Dressing (recipe follows)

3 large heads garlic, cloves peeled

2 teaspoons olive oil

1 pound slender Asian eggplants, halved lengthwise and cut into thirds

1 package (about 9 oz.) fresh cheese tortellini or ravioli

2 tablespoons chopped parsley

24 to 32 spinach leaves, coarse stems removed, rinsed and crisped

Salt and pepper

1. Prepare Balsamic Vinegar Dressing; set aside.

2. Mix garlic and 1 teaspoon of the oil in a lightly oiled 8-inch baking pan. Rub eggplant skins with remaining oil and arrange, skin sides down, in a lightly oiled 10 by 15-inch baking pan.

3. Bake garlic and eggplants in a 475° oven, switching pan positions halfway through baking, until garlic is tinged with brown (remove cloves as they brown) and eggplants are richly browned and soft when pressed (20 to 30 minutes); if drippings begin to burn, add 4 to 6 tablespoons water, stirring to loosen browned bits. Meanwhile, bring 12 cups water to a boil in a pan over medium-high heat. Stir in pasta and cook just until tender to bite.

4. Drain pasta and transfer to bowl. Add bell peppers, garlic, eggplants, parsley, and dressing. Mix thoroughly, but gently. Arrange spinach on 4 individual plates. Spoon on pasta mixture.

makes 4 servings

BALSAMIC VINEGAR DRESSING

In a small bowl, combine 2 tablespoons reduced-sodium soy sauce, 2 teaspoons balsamic vinegar, 1 teaspoon Asian sesame oil, and ½ teaspoon honey. Beat until blended.

per serving: 445 calories, 19 g protein, 75 g carbohydrates, 10 g total fat, 28 mg cholesterol, 844 mg sodium

sweet spice meat sauce

preparation time: about 20 minutes
cooking time: about 1 2/3 hours

Spice Blend (recipe follows)

4 slices bacon, chopped

1 pound lean ground beef

4 medium-size onions, chopped

1 cup finely chopped celery

2 cloves garlic, minced or pressed

2 tablespoons minced parsley

3 cans (about 15 oz. *each*) tomato sauce

1 can (about 6 oz.) tomato paste

2 tablespoons red wine vinegar

1. Prepare Spice Blend.

2. Combine bacon and beef in a 5- to 6-quart pan. Cook over medium-high heat, stirring often, until well browned.

3. Pour off fat. Add onions, celery, garlic, parsley, and Spice Blend. Cook, stirring often, until onions are soft (about 20 minutes).

4. Add tomato sauce, tomato paste, and vinegar; stir well. Bring to a boil; reduce heat and simmer until reduced to about 8 cups (about 1 hour). If made ahead, let cool and then cover and refrigerate for up to 2 days; reheat before using.

makes about 8 cups

SPICE BLEND

In small bowl, combine 1 tablespoon firmly packed brown sugar; ½ teaspoon *each* ground cinnamon, dried oregano, pepper, rubbed sage, and dried thyme; and ¼ teaspoon each ground cloves and ground nutmeg. Mix until blended.

per serving: 121 calories, 7 g protein, 13 g carbohydrates, 5 g total fat, 19 mg cholesterol, 616 mg sodium

penne, tofu & asparagus

preparation time: about 35 minutes
marinating time: 15 minutes

¹/₂ **cup seasoned rice vinegar;**
   or ¹/₂ cup distilled white vinegar

4 teaspoons sugar

¹/₄ **cup freshly grated Parmesan cheese**

3 tablespoons finely chopped fresh basil
   or 1 tablespoon dried basil

2 tablespoons olive oil

1 tablespoon Dijon mustard

1 clove garlic, minced or pressed

8 ounces regular tofu, rinsed and drained,
   cut into ¹/₂-inch cubes

1 pound asparagus, tough ends removed,
   cut diagonally into 1 ¹/₂-inch pieces

8 ounces (about 2 ¹/₂ cups) dried penne

1 Combine vinegar, cheese, basil, oil, mustard, and garlic in a large serving bowl. Mix well. Add tofu and stir to coat. Cover and let stand for 15 minutes.

2 Bring 12 cups water to a boil in a 5- to 6-quart pan over medium-high heat. Add asparagus and cook until tender when pierced (about 4 minutes). Lift out with a slotted spoon, add to tofu mixture, and keep warm.

3 Stir pasta into boiling water and cook just until tender to bite (8 to 10 minutes); or cook according to package directions. Drain well. Add pasta to tofu and asparagus. Mix thoroughly but gently.

makes 6 servings

per serving: 254 calories, 11 g protein, 35 g carbohydrates, 8 g total fat, 3 mg cholesterol, 524 mg sodium

food-processor pasta

preparation time: about 30 minutes

About 2 cups all-purpose flour

2 large eggs

About ¹/₄ cup water

1 Combine 2 cups of the flour and eggs in a food processor; whirl until mixture resembles cornmeal (about 5 seconds). With motor running, pour ¹/₄ cup of the water through feed tube and whirl until dough forms a ball. Dough should be well blended but not sticky. If dough feels sticky, add a little flour and whirl to blend; if it looks crumbly, add 1 or 2 teaspoons more water: if processor begins to slow down or stop (an indication that dough is properly mixed), turn off motor and proceed to next step.

2 Turn dough out onto a floured board and knead a few times just until smooth. If you plan to use a rolling pin, cover and let rest for 20 minutes. If you plan to use a pasta machine (manual or electric), roll out at once.

3 Use a rolling pin or pasta machine to roll out and cut dough.

makes 14 to 16 ounces uncooked pasta (machine-rolled dough makes about 32 pieces lasagne or about 4 cups cooked medium-wide noodles; yield off hand-rolled pasta varies).

per ounce: 71 calories, 3 g protein, 13 g carbohydrates, 0.8 g total fat, 28 mg cholesterol, 9 mg sodium

chilled asian pasta with shrimp

preparation time: about 40 minutes

chilling time: at least 1 hour

3 tablespoons salad oil

3 cloves garlic, minced or pressed

1/3 cup thinly sliced green onions (including tops)

1/8 teaspoon ground red pepper (cayenne)

1 1/2 pounds medium-size shrimp (about 35 per lb.), shelled and deveined

3 tablespoons each dry sherry and white wine vinegar

1 tablespoon Dijon mustard

1 tablespoon finely chopped fresh tarragon leaves or 1 teaspoon dry tarragon leaves

Asian Dressing (recipe follows)

12 ounces dry whole wheat spaghetti

2 quarts watercress sprigs, rinsed and crisped

1 Heat oil in a wide frying pan over medium-high heat. Add garlic, onions, and pepper; cook, stirring often, until onions are soft (about 3 minutes). Add shrimp and cook, stirring, until opaque in center; cut to test (about 5 minutes). Add sherry, vinegar, mustard, and tarragon; bring to a boil, stirring. Transfer mixture to a bowl and let cool; then cover and refrigerate for at least 1 hour or up to 8 hours.

2 Prepare Asian Dressing and set aside.

3 In an 8- to 10-quart pan, cook pasta in 6 quarts boiling water until al dente (about 10 minutes or according to package directions). Drain, rinse with cold water until cool, and drain again. Mix lightly with dressing. (At this point, you may cover and refrigerate for up to 8 hours.)

4 Arrange watercress on a platter. Spoon pasta over watercress and top with shrimp mixture.

makes 4 to 6 servings

ASIAN DRESSING

Mix 1/3 cup lemon juice, 3 tablespoons reduced-sodium soy sauce, 1 tablespoon each sesame oil and finely chopped fresh ginger and 2 teaspoons sugar.

per serving: 487 calories, 35 g protein, 59 g carbohydrates, 14 g total fat, 168 mg cholesterol, 647 mg sodium

cool pasta shells with scallops

preparation time: about 35 minutes

chilling time: at least 2 hours

8 ounces medium-size dry pasta shells

4 cups broccoli flowerets, cut into bite-size pieces

1 pound sea scallops, rinsed, drained, and cut in half horizontally

1/4 cup each lemon juice, white wine, vinegar, and olive oil

1 teaspoon each dry mustard and sugar

1 clove garlic, minced or pressed

1 cup finely chopped fresh basil leaves

Small inner leaves from 2 large heads romaine lettuce (about 30 total), rinsed and crisped

1 In a 5- to 6-quart pan, cook pasta in 3 quarts boiling water until al dente (7 to 9 minutes or according to package directions). Drain, rinse with cold water until cool, and drain again. Set aside.

2 In a wide frying pan, cook broccoli, covered, in 1/4 inch boiling water until tender-crisp (about 4 minutes). Drain, immerse in ice water until cool, and drain again. Set aside. In same pan, cook scallops, covered, in 1/4 inch boiling water until opaque in center; cut to test (about 3 minutes). Drain; set aside.

3 In a large bowl, mix lemon juice, vinegar, oil, mustard, sugar, garlic, and basil. Add pasta, broccoli, and scallops; mix gently. Cover and refrigerate for at least 2 hours or until next day.

4 Arrange lettuce on individual plates; top with pasta mixture.

makes 4 to 6 servings

per searing: 402 calories, 26 g protein, 47 g carbohydrates, 13 g total fat, 30 mg cholesterol, 182 mg sodium

homemade egg pasta

preparation time: about 45 minutes

About 2 cups all-purpose flour

2 large eggs

3 to 6 tablespoons water

1. Mound 2 cups of the flour on a work surface or in a large bowl and make a deep well in center. Break eggs into well. With a fork, beat eggs lightly; stir in 2 tablespoons of the water. Using a circular motion, draw in flour from sides of well. Add 1 tablespoon more water and continue to mix until flour is evenly moistened. If necessary, add more water, 1 tablespoon at a time. When dough becomes too stiff to stir easily, use your hands to finish mixing.

2. Pat dough into a ball and knead a few times to help flour absorb liquid. To knead, flatten dough ball slightly and fold farthest edge toward you. With heel of your hand, push dough away from you, sealing fold. Rotate dough a quarter turn and continue folding-pushing motion, making a turn each time.

3. Clean and lightly flour work surface. If you plan to use a rolling pin, knead dough until smooth and elastic (about 10 minutes), adding flour if needed to prevent sticking. Cover and let rest for 20 minutes. If you plan to use a pasta machine (manual or electric), knead dough until no longer sticky (3 to 4 minutes), adding flour if needed to prevent sticking.

4. Use a rolling pin or pasta machine to roll out and cut dough as directed on facing page.

makes 14 to 16 ounces uncooked pasta (machine-rolled dough)

makes about 32 pieces lasagne or about 4 cups cooked medium-wide noodles; (yield of hand-rolled pasta varies)

per ounce: 71 calories, 3 g protein, 13 g carbohydrates, 0.8 g total fat, 28 mg cholesterol, 9 mg sodium

noodles with cabbage & gruyère

preparation time: about 30 minutes

1 cup low-sodium chicken broth

1 head green cabbage, finely shredded

12 ounces dry whole wheat spaghetti

1 1/2 teaspoons caraway seeds

2 ounces Gruyère cheese, grated

4 ounces thinly sliced prosciutto, fat trimmed, cut into slivers

1. In a 4- to 5-quart pan, combine chicken broth and cabbage. Cover and bring to a boil over high heat; reduce heat and simmer, stirring occasionally, until cabbage is very tender (about 15 minutes). Uncover, increase heat to high, and continue cooking, stirring often, until most of the liquid is absorbed (3 to 5 more minutes).

2. Meanwhile, cook pasta in 6 quarts boiling water in an 8- to 10-quart pan until al dente (9 to 12 minutes or according to package directions).

3. Drain pasta and place in a large, warm bowl. Add cabbage mixture, caraway seeds, Gruyère, and prosciutto; mix well.

makes 4 servings

per serving: 446 calories, 26 g protein, 72 g carbohydrates, 9 g total fat, 32 mg cholesterol, 696 mg sodium

pasta with lentils and oranges

preparation time: about 50 minutes

4 or 5 large oranges

8 large butter lettuce leaves, rinsed and crisped

1 tablespoon grated orange peel

³/₄ cup fresh orange juice

3 tablespoons chopped fresh basil
   or 1 tablespoon dried basil

3 tablespoons white wine vinegar

1 tablespoon *each* honey and Dijon mustard

2 to 3 cloves garlic, minced or pressed

1 ¹/₂ teaspoons ground cumin

¹/₈ teaspoon crushed red pepper flakes
   (or to taste)

2 cups vegetable broth

³/₄ cup lentils

12 ounces dried radiatorre or fusilli

Basil sprigs

1. Cut peel and all white membrane from orange. Coarsely chop one of the oranges and set aside. Thinly slice remaining 3 or 4 oranges crosswise. Arrange lettuce leaves in a wide, shallow bowl or on a rimmed platter. Top with orange slices; cover and set aside.

2. In a small bowl, stir together chopped orange, orange peel, orange juice, 2 tablespoons of the chopped basil (or 2 teaspoons of the dried basil), vinegar, honey, mustard, garlic, cumin, and red pepper flakes. Beat until blended; set aside.

3. In a 1¹/₂- to 2-quart pan, bring broth to a boil over medium-high heat. Sort through lentils, discarding any debris; rinse, drain, and add to pan along with remaining 1 tablespoon chopped basil (or 1 teaspoon dried basil). Reduce heat, cover, and simmer until lentils are tender to bite (about 25 minutes).

4. Meanwhile, in a 5- to 6-quart pan, bring about 3 quarts water to a boil over medium-high heat; stir in pasta and cook until just until tender to bite 8 to 10 minutes); or cook pasta according to package directions.

5. Drain pasta well; if necessary, drain lentils well. Transfer pasta and lentils to a large bowl. Add orange dressing and mix gently but thoroughly. Spoon pasta over orange slices. Garnish with basil sprigs.

makes 4 servings

per serving: 563 calories, 21 g protein, 115 g carbohydrates, 3 g total fat, 0 mg cholesterol, 601 mg sodium

orecchiette with sake-clam sauce

preparation time: about 30 minutes

2 cans (about 6 ¹/₂ oz. *each*) chopped clams

4 cup finely chopped onions

2 cloves garlic, minced or pressed

1 cup sake or dry vermouth

2 tablespoons capers, drained

8 ounces dried orecchiette
   or other medium-size pasta shape

¹/₄ cup finely chopped parsley

¹/₄ cup freshly grated Parmesan cheese

¹/₈ teaspoon crushed red pepper flakes

1. Drain clams, reserving juice. Set clams aside.

2. Combine ½ cup of the clam juice, onions, garlic, and ¼ cup of the sake in a wide nonstick frying pan. Cook over high heat, stirring often, until about a quarter of the liquid remains (about 3 minutes). Add clams, capers, and remaining ¾ cup sake. Reduce heat and simmer, uncovered, for about 4 minutes. Remove from heat and keep warm.

3. Bring 8 cups water to a boil in a 4- to 5-quart pan over medium-high heat. Stir in pasta and cook just until tender to bite (8 to 10 minutes); or cook according to package directions. Drain well. Transfer to a wide serving bowl. Quickly add clam mixture and stir until most of the liquid is absorbed. Add parsley, cheese, and red pepper flakes. Mix thoroughly but gently.

makes 4 servings

per serving: 381 calories, 22 g protein, 49 g carbohydrates, 3 g total fat, 36 mg cholesterol, 266 mg sodium

pork tenderloin with peanut vermicelli

preparation time: about 55 minutes

2 pork tenderloins (about 12 oz. *each*), trimmed of fat and silvery membrane

¼ cup hoisin sauce

3 tablespoons firmly packed brown sugar

2 tablespoons dry sherry

2 tablespoons reduced-sodium soy sauce

1 tablespoon lemon juice

12 ounces dried vermicelli

½ cup plum jam or plum butter

¼ cup seasoned rice vinegar; or ¼ cup distilled white vinegar and 2 teaspoons sugar

¼ cup creamy peanut butter

3 tablespoons Asian sesame oil

2 cloves garlic, minced or pressed

⅛ teaspoon ground ginger

¼ teaspoon crushed red pepper flakes

1 package (about 10 oz.) frozen tiny peas, thawed

⅓ cup cilantro

2 tablespoons chopped peanuts (optional)

Sliced kumquats (optional)

1. Place tenderloins on a rack in a 9- by 13-inch baking pan. In a bowl, stir together hoisin, brown sugar, sherry, 1 tablespoon of the soy sauce, and lemon juice. Brush over pork, reserving remaining mixture.

2. Roast pork in a 450° oven, brushing with remaining marinade, until a meat thermometer inserted in thickest part registers 155° (20 to 30 minutes; after 15 minutes, check temperature every 5 minutes); if drippings begin to burn, add 4 to 6 tablespoons water, stirring to loosen browned bits. Meanwhile, bring 12 cups water to a boil in a 5- to 6-quart pan over medium-high heat. Stir in pasta and cook just until tender to bite (8 to 10 minutes); or cook according to package directions. Drain well and keep warm.

3. Transfer meat to a board, cover loosely, and let stand for 10 minutes. Skim and discard fat from pan drippings. Pour drippings and any juices on board into a small serving container; keep warm. Meanwhile, combine jam, vinegar, peanut butter, oil, garlic, ginger, red pepper flakes, and remaining 1 tablespoon soy sauce in 5- to 6-quart pan. Bring to a boil over medium heat and cook, whisking, just until smooth. Remove from heat and add pasta, peas, and cilantro. Lift with 2 forks to mix. Mound pasta on individual plates. Thinly slice meat across grain; arrange on pasta. Garnish with kumquats, if desired. Offer juices and, if desired, peanuts to add to taste.

makes 6 servings

per serving: 631 calories, 37 g protein, 80 g carbohydrates, 18 g total fat, 67 mg cholesterol, 919 mg sodium

START PASTA WATER FIRST: When you're cooking pasta, your first step should be to heat the water—it takes time for a large quantity of water to boil. If the water comes to a rolling boil before you need to cook your pasta, reduce the heat to keep it at a simmer. Just before you want to cook, increase the heat again; the water will return to a boil fairly rapidly.

linguini with creamy shrimp

preparation time: about 35 minutes

3 tablespoons sun-dried tomatoes packed in oil,
   drained (reserve oil) and chopped

1 clove garlic, minced or pressed

1 pound large shrimp (31 to 35 per lb.),
   shelled and deveined

10 ounces dried linguine

2/3 cup light cream

1/4 cup thinly sliced green onions

2 tablespoons chopped fresh basil
   or 1 teaspoon dried basil

1/8 teaspoon ground white pepper

2 teaspoons cornstarch blended
   with 3/4 cup nonfat milk

3 tablespoons dry vermouth, or to taste

Freshly grated Parmesan cheese

Salt

1. Heat 1 teaspoon of the reserved oil from tomatoes in a wide nonstick frying pan over medium high heat. Add garlic and shrimp. Cook, stirring often, just until shrimp are opaque in center, cut to test (about 6 minutes). Lift out and set aside, reserving any juices in pan.

2. Bring 12 cups water to a boil in a 5- to 6-quart pan over medium-high heat. Stir in pasta and cook just until tender to bite (8 to 10 minutes); or cook according to package directions.

3. Meanwhile, combine cream, onions, basil, tomatoes, and white pepper with juices in frying pan. Bring to a boil over medium-high heat and cook, stirring, for 1 minute. Stir cornstarch mixture and add to pan. Return mixture to a boil and cook, stirring, just until slightly thickened. Remove from heat; stir in vermouth and shrimp.

4. Drain pasta well and arrange on 4 individual plates. Top with shrimp mixture. Offer Parmesan cheese and salt to add to taste.

makes 4 servings

per serving: 546 calories, 31 g protein, 62 g carbohydrates, 17 g total fat, 167 mg cholesterol, 188 mg sodium

tortellini & peas in creamy lemon sauce

preparation time: about 35 minutes

1 large lemon (about 5 oz.)

1 tablespoon margarine

1/4 cup minced shallots or onion

2 tablespoons all-purpose flour

1 1/2 cups lowfat (2%) milk

1 cup fresh or frozen peas

1 package (9 oz.) fresh cheese-filled tortellini

2 tablespoons grated Parmesan cheese,
   plus additional cheese to taste

1. Grate 1 tablespoon zest (colored part of peel) from lemon. Squeeze juice. Combine in a small bowl; set aside.

2. In a 3- to 4-quart pan, melt margarine over medium heat. Add shallots and cook, stirring, until soft (about 3 minutes). Add flour and cook, stirring, for 1 minute. Add milk, increase heat to medium-high, and cook, stirring often, until sauce is thickened (about 10 minutes). Stir about 1/2 cup of the sauce into lemon mixture; return mixture to pan and stir well. Remove from heat and set aside.

3. In a 5- to 6-quart pan, cook peas and pasta in 3 quarts boiling water until peas are tender and pasta is al dente (4 to 5 minutes or according to package directions). Drain; add to pan with lemon sauce. Cook over low heat, stirring, for 2 minutes.

4. Stir in the 2 tablespoons Parmesan and offer with additional Parmesan.

makes 4 servings

per serving: 333 calories, 18 g protein, 46 g carbohydrates, 9 g total fat, 45 mg cholesterol, 424 mg sodium

italian sausage lasagne

preparation time: about 25 minutes
cooking time: about 2 hours

Low-fat Italian sausage

3 large onions, chopped

2 large stalks celery, chopped

2 medium-size carrots, chopped

5 cups beef broth

1 can (about 6 oz.) tomato paste

1 ½ teaspoons dried basil

½ teaspoon dried rosemary

¼ teaspoon ground nutmeg

12 ounces dry lasagne noodles

3 tablespoons cornstarch

1 ½ cups nonfat milk

2 cups shredded fontina cheese

½ cup freshly grated Parmesan cheese

1 Prepare Low-fat Italian Sausage; refrigerate, covered.

2 Combine onions, celery, carrots, and 1½ cups of the broth in a 5- to 6-quart pan (preferably nonstick). Bring to a boil over high heat and cook, stirring occasionally, until liquid has evaporated and vegetables begin to brown (12 to 15 minutes). To deglaze pan, add ¼ cup water, stirring to loosen browned bits. Continue to cook, stirring often, until mixture begins to brown again. Repeat deglazing step, adding ¼ cup more water each time, until mixture is richly browned.

3 Crumble sausage into pan; add ½ cup more water. Cook, stirring occasionally, until liquid has evaporated and meat begins to brown (about 10 minutes). Add ⅓ cup more water and cook, stirring, until meat is browned (2 to 4 more minutes). Reduce heat to medium-low and add 2½ cups more broth, stirring to loosen browned bits. Add tomato paste, basil, rosemary, and nutmeg. Bring to a boil; reduce heat, cover, and simmer, stirring occasionally, until flavors have blended (about 20 minutes). Meanwhile, bring 12 cups water to a boil in a 5- to 6-quart pan over medium-high heat. Stir in pasta and cook just until barely tender to bite (about 8 minutes). Drain well and keep warm.

4 Blend remaining 1 cup broth with cornstarch and milk until smooth. Add to meat mixture. Cook over medium-high heat, stirring, until bubbling and thickened. Stir in 1 cup of the fontina; remove from heat. Gently stir in pasta. Transfer to a shallow 3-quart baking dish; swirl pasta. Sprinkle with Parmesan and remaining 1 cup fontina. (At this point, you may cool, cover, and refrigerate for up to a day.)

5 Bake in a 375° oven until bubbling (about 30 minutes; 35 to 40 minutes if chilled).

makes 8 servings

per serving: 480 calories, 32 g protein, 53 g carbohydrates, 14 g total fat, 76 mg cholesterol, 1,625 mg sodium

chicken vermicelli carbonara

preparation time: about 55 minutes

1 large onion, finely chopped

$^1/_2$ teaspoon fennel seeds

1 $^3/_4$ cups low sodium chicken broth

12 to 14 ounces boneless, skinless chicken thighs, trimmed of fat and cut into $^1/_2$-inch chunks

1 cup finely chopped parsley

9 egg whites (about 6 tablespoons)

1 egg

12 ounces to 1 pound dry vermicelli

1 $^1/_2$ cups (about 6 oz.) finely shredded Parmesan cheese

Salt and freshly ground pepper

1 In a wide nonstick frying pan, combine onion, fennel seeds, and 1 cup of the broth. Bring to a boil; boil, stirring occasionally, until liquid has evaporated. Continue to cook until browned bits accumulate in pan; then add water, 2 tablespoons at a time, stirring until all browned bits are loosened. Continue to cook until mixture begins to brown again; repeat deglazing, using 2 tablespoons water each time, until onions are a uniformly light golden brown color.

2 To pan, add chicken and 2 tablespoons more water. Cook, stirring, until drippings begin to brown; deglaze pan with 2 tablespoons water. When pan is dry, add remaining $^3/_4$ cup broth; bring to a boil. Add parsley; keep warm over lowest heat. In a bowl, beat egg whites and egg to blend; set aside.

3 In a 6-quart pan, cook vermicelli in 4 quarts boiling water just until tender to bite (8 to 10 minutes); or cook according to package directions. Drain well.

4 Add hot pasta to pan with chicken. Pour egg mixture over pasta and at once begin lifting with 2 forks to mix well (eggs cook if you delay mixing); add 1 cup of the cheese as you mix. Pour mixture onto a warm deep platter and continue to mix until almost all broth is absorbed. Season to taste with remaining $^1/_2$ cup cheese, salt, and pepper.

makes 6 to 8 servings

per serving: 408 calories, 30 g protein, 46 g carbohydrates, 11 g total fat, 93 mg cholesterol, 491 mg sodium

orecchiette with spinach & garlic

preparation time: about 30 minutes

12 ounces orecchiette, ruote (wheels), or other dry pasta shape

3 tablespoons olive oil

6 cloves garlic, minced or pressed

$^1/_2$ teaspoon crushed red pepper flakes

$^1/_3$ cup low-sodium chicken broth

$^3/_4$ pound stemmed spinach leaves, rinsed well and coarsely chopped

Grated Parmesan cheese

1 In an 8- to 10-quart pan, cook pasta in 6 quarts boiling water until al dente (10 to 12 minutes or according to package directions).

2 Meanwhile, heat oil in a wide frying pan over medium heat. Add garlic and red pepper flakes. Cook, stirring occasionally, until garlic is slightly golden (about 2 minutes). Stir in chicken broth. Remove from heat and set aside.

3 Just before pasta is done, add spinach to pasta. Cook, stirring to distribute spinach, just until water returns to a full boil. Drain and place in a large, warm bowl.

4 Add sauce to pasta; mix well. Offer with Parmesan.

makes 4 servings

per serving: 434 calories, 14 g protein, 68 g carbohydrates, 12 g total fat, 0 mg cholesterol, 78 mg sodium

pasta with beans

preparation time: about 45 minutes

1 tablespoon olive oil

1 large carrot, finely chopped

2 celery stalks, finely chopped

1 medium-size onion, chopped

2 cloves garlic, minced or pressed

2 teaspoons dry marjoram leaves or dry
   oregano leaves

1 can (28 oz.) peeled tomatoes

1 can (about 15 ½ oz.) garbanzo beans,
   drained and rinsed

1 can (about 15 oz.) cannellini
   (white kidney beans), drained and rinsed

1 cup water

8 ounces multicolored rotelle (corkscrews)
   or other dry pasta shape

¼ cup minced parsley

Grated Parmesan cheese

1 Heat oil in a 4- to 5-quart pan over medium-high heat. Add carrot, celery, onion, and garlic. Cook, stirring often, until vegetables are soft (about 10 minutes). Add marjoram, tomatoes (break up with a spoon) and their liquid, garbanzos, cannellini, and water. Bring to a boil; reduce heat and simmer until slightly thickened (about 10 minutes).

2 About 5 minutes before sauce is done, cook pasta in 3 quarts boiling water in a 5- to 6-quart pan until slightly underdone (about 5 minutes or two-thirds of the cooking time indicated on package). Drain. Return to pan and stir in vegetable mixture. Bring to a boil; reduce heat and simmer, stirring often, until most of the liquid is absorbed and pasta is al dente (about 5 more minutes).

3 Transfer to a large, warm bowl. Sprinkle with parsley and offer with Parmesan.

makes 4 servings

per serving: 523 calories, 21 g protein, 98 g carbohydrates, 6 g total fat, 0 mg cholesterol, 1,069 mg sodium

spinach & tofu manicotti

preparation time: about 1½ hours

2 tablespoons olive oil

1 medium-size onion, chopped

3 celery stalks, chopped

2 cloves garlic, minced or pressed

2 teaspoons dry oregano leaves

2 cans (15 oz. *each*) tomato purée

1 cup *each* dry red wine and water

1 pound soft tofu, drained and rinsed

1 package (10 oz.) frozen chopped spinach,
   thawed and squeezed dry

12 dry manicotti tubes

½ cup shredded part-skim mozzarella cheese

1 Heat oil in a 4- to 5-quart pan over medium-high heat. Add onion, celery, garlic, and oregano. Cook, stirring often, until onion is limp (about 7 minutes). Add tomato purée, wine, and water. Bring to a boil; reduce heat, cover, and simmer for 25 minutes, stirring often.

2 Meanwhile, mix tofu and spinach in a bowl. Stuff manicotti with mixture.

3 Spread 1¾ cups of the tomato sauce in a 9- by 13-inch baking pan. Set manicotti in sauce; top with remaining sauce. Cover and bake in a 375° oven until pasta is tender (about 50 minutes). Sprinkle with mozzarella.

makes 6 servings (2 manicotti each)

per serving: 293 calories, 14 g protein, 43 g carbohydrates, 9 g total fat, 5 mg cholesterol, 672 mg sodium

vermicelli with vegetable sauce

preparation time: about 1 hour and 10 minutes

2 tablespoons olive oil or salad oil

1 medium-size onion, finely chopped

1 teaspoon *each* fennel seeds and dry basil, dry tarragon, and dry oregano leaves

1 clove garlic, minced or pressed

1 small zucchini, thinly sliced

¼ pound mushrooms, thinly sliced

1 small green bell pepper, stemmed, seeded, and finely chopped

½ cup dry red wine

1 pound tomatoes, peeled, seeded, and chopped

1 can (6 oz.) tomato paste

1 teaspoon sugar

12 ounces dry vermicelli (not coiled) or spaghettini

Grated Parmesan cheese

1. Heat oil in a 4- to 5-quart pan over medium-high heat. Add onion, fennel seeds, basil, tarragon, and oregano. Cook, stirring often, until onion is soft (about 5 minutes). Stir in garlic, zucchini, mushrooms, and bell pepper. Cook, stirring often, until mushrooms begin to brown (about 10 minutes). Add wine, tomatoes, tomato paste, and sugar. Increase heat to high and bring to a boil; reduce heat, cover, and simmer until thickened (about 35 minutes), stirring occasionally.

2. About 10 minutes before sauce is done, cook pasta in 6 quarts boiling water in an 8- to 10-quart pan until al dente (7 to 9 minutes or according to package directions).

3. Drain pasta and arrange on warm plates; top with sauce. Offer with Parmesan.

makes 4 servings

per serving: 466 calories, 15 g protein, 83 g carbohydrates, 9 g total fat, 0 mg cholesterol, 355 mg sodium

turkey italian sausage sauce

preparation time: about 50 minutes

1 pound mild or hot turkey Italian sausages, casings removed, or Low-fat Italian sausage

1 large onio, chopped

3 cloves garlic, minced or pressed

1 can (about 29 oz.) tomato purée

3 tablespoons chopped fresh basil or 1 tablespoon dried basil

½ teaspoon fennel seeds

2 tablespoons dry red wine (or to taste)

Salt and pepper

1. Chop or crumble sausages. Place in a 4- to 5-quart pan with onion, garlic, and 2 tablespoons water. Cook over medium heat, stirring often, until sausage mixture is well browned (about 15 minutes); if pan appears dry or sausage mixture sticks to pan bottom, add water, 1 tablespoon at a time.

2. Stir in tomato purée, basil, and fennel seeds. Increase heat to medium high and bring to a boil; reduce heat and simmer until reduced to about 4 ½ cups (about 20 minutes).

3. Remove from heat and add wine. Season to taste with salt and pepper. If made ahead, let cool and then cover and refrigerate for up to 2 days; reheat before using.

makes about 4 ½ cups

per serving: 54 calories, 2 g protein, 12 g carbohydrates, 0.2 g total fat, 0 mg cholesterol, 366 mg sodium

capellini with cilantro pesto & white beans

preparation time: about 35 minutes

3 cups firmly packed cilantro leaves

1 cup grated Parmesan cheese

1 tablespoon grated lemon peel

1 tablespoon Asian sesame oil

3 cloves garlic, peeled

2 teaspoons honey

8 ounces dried capellini

2 tablespoons seasoned rice vinegar
(or 2 tablespoons distilled white vinegar
plus ³/₄ teaspoon sugar)

1 medium-size red onion, cut into thin slivers

1 tablespoon balsamic vinegar

1 can (about 15 oz.) cannellini (white kidney
beans), drained and rinsed

7 medium-size firm-ripe pear-shaped (Roma-
type) tomatoes (about 1 lb. total), chopped

1 ¹/₂ teaspoons chopped fresh thyme
or ¹/₂ teaspoon dried thyme

Thyme and cilantro sprigs

Pepper

1 To prepare cilantro pesto, in a blender or a processor, combine cilantro leaves, Parmesan, ¹/₂ cup water, lemon peel, sesame oil, garlic, and honey. Whirl until smoothly puréed. If pesto is too thick, add a little more water, set aside. (At this point, you may cover and refrigerate for up to 3 hours; bring to room temperature before using.)

2 In a 4- to 5-quart pan, cook pasta in about 8 cups boiling water until just tender to bite (about 3 minutes); or cook according to package directions. Drain well, rinse with hot water, and drain well again. Quickly return pasta to pan; add rice vinegar and lift with 2 forks to mix. Keep warm.

3 While pasta is cooking, combine onion and ¹/₃ cup water in a wide nonstick frying pan or wok. Cover and cook over medium-high heat until onion is almost soft (about 3 minutes). Uncover, add balsamic vinegar, and stir-fry until liquid has evaporated. Add beans, tomatoes, and chopped thyme to pan; stir-fry gently until beans are heated through and tomatoes are soft (about 3 minutes). Remove pan from heat.

4 Stir cilantro pesto well; spread evenly on 4 individual plates. Top with pasta, then with bean mixture. Garnish with thyme and cilantro sprigs; serve immediately. Season to taste with pepper.

makes 4 servings

per serving: 473 calories, 20 g protein, 73 g carbohydrates, 11 g total fat, 16 mg cholesterol, 786 mg sodium

INTERNATIONAL BREADS : Good bread enhances any meal, whether it encloses sandwich makings or serves as a side dish to soups, salads, or other entrées. Many traditionalists prefer crusty rolls or French bread baguettes, but a delicatessen, well-stocked supermarket, or ethnic bakery offers many tempting alternatives.If your meal has an international theme, choose a complementary bread. Try flat, chewy focaccia or seasoned breadsticks with Italian dishes, warm corn or flour tortillas with Mexican favorites; offer crisp flatbread with Scandinavian specialties, dense pumpernickel with German dishes. Armenian cracker bread or pita bread enhances Middle Eastern entrées, while challah and onion rolls go well with Jewish meals.

summertime pasta alfresco

preparation time: about 35 minutes
chilling time: at least 2 hours

3 small tomatoes, peeled and chopped

1 cup each thinly sliced green onions (including tops), finely chopped

Celery, finely chopped green bell pepper, and diced zucchini

2 cloves garlic, minced or pressed

3 tablespoons white wine vinegar

1 tablespoon sugar

$1/3$ cup chopped fresh basil leaves

1 teaspoon chopped fresh rosemary

$3/4$ teaspoon chopped fresh oregano leaves

Coarsely ground pepper

8 ounces rotelle (corkscrews), ruote (wheels), or other dry pasta shape

2 tablespoons grated Parmesan cheese

1. Combine tomatoes, onions, celery, bell pepper, zucchini, garlic, vinegar, sugar, basil, rosemary, and oregano. Season to taste with pepper; mix well. Cover and refrigerate for at least 2 hours or up to 8 hours.

2. Shortly before serving, cook pasta in 3 quarts boiling water in a 5- to 6-quart pan until al dente (7 to 9 minutes or according to package directions). Drain, rinse with cold water until cool, and drain again.

3. Transfer pasta to a serving bowl. Add tomato mixture and mix lightly. Sprinkle with Parmesan and mix again.

makes 4 servings

per serving: 283 calories, 11 g protein, 56 g carbohydrates, 2 g total fat, 2 mg cholesterol, 97 mg sodium

red pepper pesto

preparation time: 10 minutes

1 jar (12 oz.) roasted red peppers, drained, patted dry

1 cup lightly packed fresh basil leaves

1 clove garlic, peeled

$1/3$ cup grated Parmesan cheese

Salt and pepper

In a food processor or blender, whirl peppers, basil, garlic, and cheese until basil is finely chopped. Season to taste with salt and pepper.

makes about 1 $1/2$ cups

per tablespoon: 14 calories, 0.7 g protein, 2 g carbohydrates, 0.4 g total fat, 0.9 mg cholesterol, 51 mg sodium

perciatelli with turkey marinara

preparation time: about 20 minutes
cooking time: about 1 hour and 40 minutes

2 tablespoons olive oil

1 medium-size onion, finely chopped

1 medium-size green bell pepper,
   stemmed, seeded, and finely chopped

1 large carrot, finely shredded

1/4 pound mushrooms, thinly sliced

2 tablespoons chopped parsley

1 clove garlic, minced or pressed

2 teaspoons dry basil leaves

1 teaspoon *each* dry rosemary
   and dry oregano leaves

1 pound fresh ground turkey

2 cans (28 oz. *each*) peeled tomatoes

1 can (12 oz.) tomato paste

1/4 cup dry red wine

1 bay leaf

1 pound perciatelli, bucatini,
   or other dry pasta noodles

Grated Parmesan cheese

1 Heat oil in a 4- to 5-quart pan over medium-high heat. Add onion, bell pepper, carrot, mushrooms, parsley, garlic, basil, rosemary, and oregano. Cook, stirring often, until vegetables are tender (about 15 minutes). Lift out and set aside.

2 Crumble turkey into pan; cook over medium-high heat, stirring constantly, until lightly browned (about 7 minutes). Pour off fat. Return vegetables to pan. Stir in tomatoes (break up with a spoon) and their liquid, tomato paste, wine, and bay leaf. Bring to a boil; reduce heat, cover, and simmer, stirring occasionally, for 30 minutes. Uncover and continue cooking, stirring occasionally, until sauce is thickened (about 45 more minutes).

3 About 10 minutes before sauce is done, cook pasta in 6 quarts boiling water in an 8- to 10-quart pan until al dente (7 to 9 minutes or according to package directions).

4 Drain pasta and place in a large, warm bowl. Add sauce and mix lightly. Offer with Parmesan.

makes 6 to 8 servings

per serving: 497 calories, 25 g protein, 73 g carbohydrates, 13 g total fat, 33 mg cholesterol, 809 mg sodium

mint pesto

preparation time: 15 minutes

1/2 cup pine nuts

1 cup lightly packed fresh mint leaves

3 cloves garlic, peeled

3 tablespoons olive oil

1/4 cup grated Parmesan cheese

1 Stir pine nuts in a wide frying pan over medium heat until golden (about 3 minutes). Pour into a food processor or blender; let cool slightly.

2 To pine nuts, add mint, garlic, oil, and cheese. Whirl until smoothly puréed.

makes about 3/4 cup

per tablespoon: 71 calories, 2 g protein, 1 g carbohydrates, 7 g total fat, 1 mg cholesterol, 31 mg sodium

bow tie pasta with broccoli pesto

preparation time: about 35 minutes

1 pound broccoli flowerets

2 or 3 cloves garlic, minced or pressed

$^1/_2$ cup grated Parmesan cheese

3 tablespoons olive oil

1 $^1/_2$ teaspoons Asian sesame oil

$^1/_2$ teaspoon salt

12 ounces dried pasta bow ties (farfalle)

1 to 2 tablespoons seasoned rice vinegar (or 1 to 2 tablespoons distilled white vinegar plus $^1/_2$ to 1 teaspoon sugar)

1 small tomato, chopped

1. In a 4- to 5-quart pan, bring 8 cups water to a boil over medium-high heat. Stir in broccoli and cook until just tender to bite (about 7 minutes). Immediately drain broccoli, immerse in ice water until cool, and drain again.

2. In a food processor or blender, combine a third of the broccoli with garlic, cheese, olive oil, sesame oil, salt, and 3 tablespoons water. Whirl until smooth. Scrape down sides of container, add half the remaining broccoli, and whirl until smooth again. Add remaining broccoli; whirl until smooth. Set aside.

3. In a 5- to 6-quart pan, bring about 3 quarts water to a boil over medium high heat; stir in pasta and cook until just tender to bite, 8 to 10 minutes. (Or cook pasta according to package directions.)

4. Drain pasta well. Transfer to a large serving bowl and stir in vinegar. Add pesto and mix gently but thoroughly. Garnish with tomato and serve immediately.

makes 4 servings

per serving: 510 calories, 19 g protein, 73 g carbohydrates, 17 g total fat, 8 mg cholesterol, 604 mg sodium

sausage, basil & port fettuccine

preparation time: about 45 minutes

1 pound mild or hot pork Italian sausages (casings removed), crumbled into $^1/_2$-inch pieces

2 cloves garlic, minced or pressed

1 $^1/_2$ cups sliced green onions

3 cups thinly sliced red onions

1 $^1/_2$ cups port

3 medium-size tomatoes, chopped

2 tablespoons balsamic vinegar

$^3/_4$ cup chopped fresh basil

1 pound dried fettuccine

Basil sprigs

1. In a wide nonstick frying pan or wok, stir-fry sausage over medium-high heat until browned (7 to 10 minutes). Remove from pan with a slotted spoon; keep warm. Pour off and discard all but 1 teaspoon fat from pan.

2. Add garlic, green onions, and red onions to pan and stir-fry until soft (5 to 7 minutes). Add water, 1 tablespoon at a time; if pan appears dry. Add port and bring to a boil. Then boil, stirring often, until liquid is reduced by half (5 to 6 minutes). Add tomatoes, vinegar, and sausage; reduce heat and simmer for 2 minutes. Stir in chopped basil.

3. While sauce is cooking, in a 6- to 8-quart pan, cook fettuccine in about 4 quarts boiling water until just tender to bite (8 to 10 minutes); or cook according to package directions.

4. Drain pasta well and transfer to a warm bowl; top with sausage sauce. Garnish with basil sprigs.

makes 8 servings

per serving: 473 calories, 18 g protein, 58 g carbohydrates, 14 g total fat, 87 mg cholesterol, 417 mg sodium

seafood linguine

preparation time: about 50 minutes

2 pounds mussels or small hard-shell clams in shells, scrubbed

1 bottle (8 oz.) clam juice

4 tablespoons margarine

3/4 cup sliced green onions (including tops)

2 large cloves garlic, minced or pressed

1/2 cup dry white wine

1 pound medium-size shrimp (about 35 *total*), shelled and deveined

12 ounces fresh linguine

1/2 cup chopped parsley

1. If using mussels, discard any that don't close when lightly tapped. With a swift tug, pull beard (clump of fibers along side of shell) off each mussel.

2. Pour clam juice into a 5- to 6-quart pan and bring to a boil over high heat. Add mussels; reduce heat to medium, cover, and cook until shells open (about 8 minutes). Discard any unopened shells. Drain, reserving liquid. Set mussels aside and keep warm. Strain cooking liquid to remove grit; reserve 1 cup of the liquid.

3. In a wide frying pan, melt 2 tablespoons of the margarine over medium-high heat. Add onions and garlic and cook, stirring often, until onions are soft (about 3 minutes). Stir in wine and reserved cooking liquid. Increase heat to high and bring to a boil; cook until reduced by about half (about 5 minutes). Stir in remaining margarine. Add shrimp, cover, and remove from heat; let stand until shrimp are opaque in center; cut to test (about 8 minutes).

4. Meanwhile, cook pasta in 6 quarts boiling water in an 8- to 10-quart pan until al dente (3 to 4 minutes or according to package directions). Drain.

5. Add pasta and parsley to shrimp mixture and mix lightly, lifting pasta with 2 forks. Mound on a warm platter; add mussels.

makes 6 servings

per serving: 342 calories, 25 g protein, 35 g carbohydrates, 719 total fat, 247 mg cholesterol, 410 mg sodium

winter garden pasta

preparation time: about 40 minutes

3/4 pound Swiss chard, rinsed and drained

2 tablespoons olive oil

1 pound mushrooms, sliced

1 medium-size onion, chopped

3 cloves garlic, minced or pressed

1/2 cup low-sodium chicken broth

1 1/2 pounds pear-shaped tomatoes, chopped

Freshly ground pepper

1 pound penne, rigatoni, or other dry pasta shape

Grated Parmesan cheese

1. Trim off and discard discolored ends of Swiss chard stems. Cut white stalks from leaves. Finely chop leaves and stalks separately. Set leaves aside.

2. Heat oil in a wide frying pan over medium high heat. Stir in chard stalks, mushrooms, onion, and garlic; cover and cook until vegetables are soft (about 10 minutes). Uncover and cook, stirring, until liquid has evaporated (about 3 minutes).

3. Add chicken broth and chard leaves; cover and cook until leaves are wilted (about 2 minutes). Stir in tomatoes and season to taste with pepper. Cover, remove from heat, and set aside.

4. In an 8- to 10-quart pan, cook pasta in 6 quarts boiling water until al dente (7 to 9 minutes or ac cording to package directions).

5. Drain pasta and place in a large, warm bowl. Add chard mixture; mix well. Offer with Parmesan.

makes 4 to 6 servings

per serving: 455 calories, 16 g protein, 82 g carbohydrates, 8 g total fat, 0 mg cholesterol, 171 mg sodium

vegetable lasagne

preparation time: about 1 ¼ hours

1 pound firm tofu

1 package (8 oz.) dry lasagne noodles

1 pound carrots, cut into ¼-inch-thick slices

1 pound zucchini, cut into ¼-inch-thick slices

1 tablespoon olive oil or salad oil

1 large onion, chopped

1 pound mushrooms, thinly sliced

1 teaspoon *each* dry basil, dry thyme leaves, and dry oregano leaves

2 large cans (15 oz. *each*) no-salt-added tomato sauce

1 can (6 oz.) tomato paste

2 packages (10 oz. *each*) frozen chopped spinach, thawed and squeezed dry

1 cup part-skim ricotta cheese

2 cups shredded skim mozzarella cheese

1 cup grated Parmesan cheese

1 Break tofu into coarse chunks and drain in a colander. With paper towels, press tofu to remove excess liquid. Set aside.

2 In a 5- to 6-quart pan, bring 3 quarts water to a boil over high heat. Add noodles and carrots; cook for 6 minutes. Add zucchini; continue to cook until noodles are just tender to bite (about 4 more minutes). Drain well; set vegetables and noodles aside separately.

3 Heat oil in same pan over medium-high heat. Add tofu, onion, mushrooms, basil, thyme, and oregano. Cook, stirring often, until onion is soft and liquid has evaporated (about 7 minutes). Add tomato sauce and tomato paste; stir to blend, then set aside. Mix spinach and ricotta cheese; set aside.

4 Spread a third of the sauce in a 9- by 13-inch baking dish. Arrange half the noodles over sauce; sprinkle evenly with half each of the carrots, zucchini, spinach mixture, and mozzarella cheese. Repeat layers; then spread remaining sauce on top. Sprinkle with Parmesan cheese.

5 Set baking dish in a rimmed baking pan to catch any drips. Bake, uncovered, in a 400° oven until hot in center (about 25 minutes). Let stand for 5 minutes before serving.

makes 6 servings

per serving: 602 calories, 41 g protein, 70 g carbohydrates, 21 g total fat, 36 mg cholesterol, 654 mg sodium

basil pesto

preparation time: 10 minutes

2 cups lightly packed fresh basil leaves

½ cup grated Parmesan cheese

⅓ cup olive oil

¼ cup walnut pieces

2 cloves garlic, peeled

In a food processor or blender, whirl basil, cheese, oil, walnuts, and garlic until smoothly puréed.

makes about 1 cup

per tablespoon: 69 calories, 2 g protein, 2 g carbohydrates, 6 g total fat, 2 mg cholesterol, 48 mg sodium

index